The Light at the End of the Tunnel

Coming Back to Life After a Spouse Dies

By
Mary Ward Menke

Bloomington, IN Milton Keynes, UK

authorHOUSE

AuthorHouse™
1663 Liberty Drive, Suite 200
Bloomington, IN 47403
www.authorhouse.com
Phone: 1-800-839-8640

AuthorHouse™ UK Ltd.
500 Avebury Boulevard
Central Milton Keynes, MK9 2BE
www.authorhouse.co.uk
Phone: 08001974150

First published by AuthorHouse 7/12/2006

ISBN: 1-4259-4421-3 (sc)

Library of Congress Control Number: 2006905330

*Printed in the United States of America
Bloomington, Indiana*

This book is printed on acid-free paper.

ACKNOWLEDGEMENTS

I started collecting these stories of survival four years ago, shortly after my friend's husband died. Some of the stories are from family and friends, but many are from strangers—people who responded to my internet-based request. I am deeply appreciative to each one for willingly reopening wounds and sharing their pain and ultimate recoveries with people they will never meet, but with whom they share a special bond.

Most of the stories are followed by a brief biography of the author. However, I was unable to contact several authors after all the stories were compiled and edited. To them I apologize.

TABLE OF CONTENTS

Introduction

We're all familiar with those words from marriage vows: "Till death do us part." But how many of us stop to consider what those words really mean? And why should we be expected to dwell on future sadness on what is meant to be one of the happiest days of our lives?

The truth is, "till death do us part" is something we pay lip service to. We know intellectually what the words mean, but no one wants to believe it will happen to us. Sure, everyone will die—eventually—at a time too far off to even contemplate, but why worry about it now?

Unfortunately, it's a sad fact that half of us will eventually have to face the death of a spouse. But just as no two relationships are exactly alike, there is no right or wrong way to grieve this loss. Yes, there are myriad advice books from experts—psychologists, psychiatrists, clergy, etc.—detailing the necessary steps of grieving, but too often widows or widowers read these books and think they're not doing it "right" because they haven't experienced all those steps in exactly those ways.

The Light at the End of the Tunnel: Coming Back to Life After a Spouse Dies contains real-life stories from survivors—those who have actually experienced the death of a spouse. Some are young, some are older; some spouses died after lengthy illnesses, some were taken suddenly; some survivors bounced back quickly, others took a while. What they have in common is that they survived and they did it their own way at their own pace, and they learned that there is no right or wrong way.

Although I am not a survivor per se, my experience comes from watching two people close to me go through the process in very different ways. My son was 23 when his wife died quite unexpectedly from a pulmonary embolism. Several years later, my best friend's husband (who also happened to be my husband's best friend) died from the same thing.

In both cases, my husband and I also were grieving, but our focus was understandably on the surviving spouses. While we had the best of intentions, we learned that sometimes our advice was offered too early, when the survivors weren't ready to hear it, and, more often than not, our suggestions might have worked for us, but not necessarily for them.

For example, I'm a joiner; my son and friend are not. I like to be around people of like minds, to listen and to share, so joining a grief support group is something I would likely be open to. My son and friend are happy with their individual group of friends and don't like to talk about their feelings except with those with whom they already have a relationship. So suggesting that they join a support group didn't ring true for either of them.

Since then, I've observed several other relatives and friends as they've traveled the road to recovery after their spouses died. It has become more and more obvious to me that individuals have to chart their own course.

That's the intention behind *The Light at the End of the Tunnel: Coming Back to Life After a Spouse Dies.* I believe that for the newly-bereaved who read these personal stories, it will become apparent that it doesn't matter *how* you go through the tunnel, as long as you come out at the other end, alive and whole—a survivor.

Mary Ward Menke
St. Louis, MO

For everything there is a season,

And a time for every matter under heaven:

A time to be born, and a time to die;

A time to plant, and a time to pluck up what is planted;

A time to kill, and a time to heal;

A time to break down, and a time to build up;

A time to weep, and a time to laugh;

A time to mourn, and a time to dance;

A time to throw away stones,

and a time to gather stones together;

A time to embrace,

And a time to refrain from embracing;

A time to seek, and a time to lose;

A time to keep, and a time to throw away;

A time to tear, and a time to sew;

A time to keep silence, and a time to speak;

A time to love, and a time to hate,

A time for war, and a time for peace.

Ecclesiastes 3:1-8

CELEBRATION

By Barbara Moorman

If, as I can't help suspecting, the dead also feel the pains of separation (and this may be one of their purgatorial sufferings), then for both lovers, and for all pairs of lovers without exception, bereavement is a universal and integral part of our experience of love.

Eleanor Roosevelt

Grief is a very private thing. And lonely. No one can do it for you. Not even really with you. They can only sympathize with what you are feeling. You can't put grief in a box. There is no predictable formula.

My husband died suddenly one March day on his way home from work. We had been planning a special celebration to be held on our soon-to-be thirty-year anniversary. He died two weeks before Easter. I absorbed the shock, even being able to continue studying toward a Master's Degree. But I was dealt a double-whammy (not from God, surely) when two weeks after my husband's death, my brother died, also suddenly, from a heart attack. My brother and I did not live in the same city so I suppose you could say I adjusted "easier" to losing him. But that's not necessarily true. Final loss is final loss.

I never felt the anger my nineteen-year old daughter did over her dad's death. I was not in denial and never asked why. I probably felt some depression, but I had great support from a "house church" group. They stuck by me and saw me through. I wrote a book about the house church which includes descriptions of a baptism, wedding, and funeral. This is what I wrote about my husband's funeral:

> *Actually, we did not have a funeral at all. It has rather been called a "memorial," which does not suffice either. Webster defines a memorial as "anything meant to help people remember some person..." We were hardly gathered to "help remember" a man who had been in our midst daily up to only four days before.*

No, truly we were *celebrating* a man's death. I and three ministers sat together one afternoon sharing our love and comforting excitement over the knowledge that this man, a minister/engineer, was alive and whole in a different dimension. We were engulfed in an electric experience. As we planned just how to celebrate new life we were stimulated, gregarious, and joyful. God's Spirit was in that room. Also, the man's spirit lingered close by thoroughly enjoying our planning. I am sure of it. He was my husband.

He and I had discussed the American-Way-of-Death, and shared the same feelings. He had willed his body to a medical school in our city. My daughter and I have, too.

At the celebration, two weeks prior to Easter, we prepared the sanctuary with hanging banners all around, one small floral arrangement, and the communion table. The organ prelude was Bach's *Sheep May Safely Graze*, which was played at our wedding. We sang hymns. We had a time for prayer, offered by any who felt so moved. Psalm 34 was read and a dear friend of ours, a dancer, moved down the center aisle toward the communion table, interpreting the Word wearing black leotards which framed her expressive body and contrasted beautifully with her white hands and face.

The breaking of bread and sharing of the cup were just that. Lines of people formed on the two outside aisles to come forward for communion. I was first and remained in the table area greeting and sharing broken bread with our dear, dear friends. It was an ecstatic, awesome, gracious celebration. God was never more present to me. The organist concluded with Handel's *Hallelujah Chorus*.

Emotional perceptions alter with years lived. Now, at the age of 85, I sometimes miss my husband afresh. I also miss my brother and other family members, and a growing number of friends. I am learning to accept loss without grieving. Sometimes I am even graced. Blessed.

Loss is one of the ways of life.

Barbara Moorman recently moved to Columbia, Missouri with her daughter after living most of her life in St. Louis, Missouri. A published author, Barbara has given up writing and now spends her free time reading and knitting.

A New Life

By Brenda Elliott

What you leave behind is not what is engraved in stone monuments, but what is woven into the lives of others.

Pericles

The date: April, 1995.

The diagnosis: Myelodysplasia

The cure: None

Date of Death: November, 1997

John Andradzki and I were married in 1959, when I was seventeen and he was nineteen. We celebrated 38 years of marriage just two months prior to his death. When he died, he had just turned 58 and I was one month shy of 56.

Myelodysplastic leukemia is a terminal blood cell-related cancer. The disease occurs when the blood-forming cells in the bone marrow produce cells that do not mature properly, leading to low counts of healthy red blood cells, white blood cells, and platelets in the blood. Red blood cells carry oxygen to all parts of the body; without oxygen all systems die. Blood transfusions may help patients with myelodysplastic leukemia for a while but they eventually lose their effectiveness.

The disease was discovered while John was undergoing pre-op blood work. He was told he might survive as long as five years; however, since there was no way of knowing how long the myelodysplasia had been present, the doctors could not accurately predict how long he would live.

I think John and I were both in shock for a while. We heard the diagnosis, heard that it was fatal, and heard there was no cure—he was going to die in five years or less—but there was a part of us that just knew there must be a mistake or that somehow a miracle would happen. That hope, slim as it was, was the very thing that kept us going and helped us cope for a while.

Neither of us wanted to accept that he was dying. Part of me knew it was true, but I felt as though I were watching from afar, like watching a movie. I felt it, I was affected by it, and yet I was detached, watching and being aware of it simultaneously. It was as if two parts of me were functioning on different levels of awareness.

I have always had a strong spiritual outlook, and this helped me get through the roughest times. I read spiritual books and tried to take care of myself, my responsibilities and my husband. I tried to keep life as normal as possible for as long as possible. We both did.

THE SIX STEPS OF THE GRIEVING PROCESS:

DENIAL: Denial came in the hope that there would be a miracle. It wasn't full-blown denial consisting of my refusal to accept the diagnosis, but rather one in which I believed that perhaps through prayer or a miracle, the disease would be arrested. I read everything I could about healing—from the traditional, to the metaphysical and alternative methodologies.

As a Reiki Master, I used Reiki (a hands-on spiritual and energetic healing technique) on him often. Though it didn't cure him, it seemed to soothe him and ease his pain and discomfort. It also allowed me to do something for him. I think in our helplessness when someone we love is ill, we want to try everything possible that we think might cure or help in an effort to take the edge off that helpless feeling.

ANGER: I cannot remember being angry until after John's death. I was angry at him for leaving me. I was lost without him, and even though I knew he didn't leave me because he wanted to, it still made me angry.

I tried to understand why John had to die so young. Oddly enough, he always told me he was going to die young. His father died at 47 and John didn't think he would live much beyond that. He outlived his father by 10 years. It felt to me like a self-fulfilling prophecy, as if he had pronounced his own death sentence. I was angry that he would do such a thing.

BARGAINING: I'm not really aware that I did any actual bargaining. I may have bargained in the sense that if I performed Reiki, or read enough books on healing, that I could have him longer or prevent his death altogether.

<u>DEPRESSION</u>: I don't think a person can live through the death of a loved one and not get depressed at times. The stress and lack of adequate rest and sleep can make a person more vulnerable to depression.

I focused on taking care of my husband, trying to continue my part-time work as a college instructor, and feeding my soul in order to keep depression at bay. After his death, the depression was probably more evident. I never required medication, though, to manage depression or even to sleep. I didn't sleep well or eat well for quite a while after his death, but I managed to get enough of both to keep going.

<u>ACCEPTANCE</u>: Acceptance played a part in the background if not in the foreground. I wanted a cure or more time with my husband, but deep inside, I knew that wasn't going to happen. Especially in those last months, the acceptance grew and I leaned even more heavily on my spiritual beliefs to get me through. John's pain was increasing, he was getting weaker, and it was becoming more and more difficult for him to breathe. I began not only to accept but to hope and pray the end would come quickly before the discomfort became unbearable for him.

After John's death, I had to accept that he was gone. The acceptance was a reqlinquishment of wanting to fight against it. I made a determined effort to start healing and go on with my life.

I seemed to experience these steps—denial, anger, bargaining, depression and acceptance—in spirals rather than in a linear fashion. They came and went in different degrees at different times. I revisited these steps again and again as I cycled through the whole process.

<u>RECOVERY</u>: I never really availed myself of a support group or counseling. I suppose I believed that as an MSW with counseling experience, I could do it alone. I did, however, call my sister-in-law several times when I needed to talk to someone who had been through it. She let me know that what I was feeling was natural and that even if I didn't think I would survive or be "normal" again, I would. I called her every time I needed to hear that again. She assured me I would "live" again because I felt very dead and almost disassociated from myself. That, I realized, was because without John, I didn't know who I was anymore.

I had a wonderful support system in friends and family, but most of all, my strong spiritual philosophy strengthened me and helped me go through the process in a fairly healthy manner.

I made an attempt to communicate with John through psychic mediums on two occasions. Prior to consulting mediums, I heard John speak to me as I was coming out of the sleep cycle one morning. I had met someone, and I heard John say to me gently that this person would not make me happy. That is the only time I thought he spoke to me. There was no such communication from him when I met my present husband, nor has there been any since then.

I had many decisions to make regarding the trust fund, our almost completely defunct business, finishing the house we started together, and moving. I went to mediums because I thought I might get some help with these decisions. I was not used to making decisions without John, and I knew nothing about handling the laundry list of things I was left to take care of. While the mediums were unable to give me specifics about what to do, I did get some reassurance that I was on the right track and that I would be fine. True or not,

I needed to hear that. I am convinced that when you believe something strongly enough, you can create it.

One medium said that John told him to ask me about the fireplace and indicated that this was to serve as proof he was in contact with me. I don't know if the medium just picked up on my thoughts or if he was indeed communicating with John, but it really doesn't matter. At the time, it seemed to make me feel better.

I finally realized that I was going to be okay a few months after John's death, through a gradual process of acceptance and getting on with my life. Even after that there were times when I would break down and cry and mourn. The episodes ended more quickly and came less often as the year wore on and even more so in the next and the next.

To the newly-bereaved, I would say, "Remember that you are an individual with individual needs and responses. I would encourage you to take advantage of counseling, especially if you do not have a good support system. We all have different strengths and weaknesses. Some of us have a stronger faith/belief/spiritual outlook than others. So, I would say use whatever works for you. I would also caution that the sooner you are able to reach acceptance, the faster you will heal. Know that you have to re-invent yourself. You won't know who you are exactly, so you have to set out to discover who you are without your mate. Find something to live for. Do things you have always wanted to do but haven't yet done."

Less than five months after John died, I made myself audition for a play at our local community theater. I hadn't done any acting since my high school play 39 years before, but I always thought I would like to act. I got a part and really threw myself into it. I also finished building the house we had started. I grabbed hold of life and refused to let go. I would assure a newly-bereaved person that life after your mate's death is possible, if you want it and are willing to work for it.

Brenda Elliott received her Bachelor's Degree in Human Service Technology from Georgia State University in Atlanta at the age of 44. She went on to obtain her Master's Degree in Social Work from the University of Georgia in Athens, Georgia three years later. After working for a while in that field, she went to work with her husband in their business and began teaching part-time for Floyd College in Rome, Georgia. She continues as a part-time instructor of Sociology for Floyd College, is active in her local little theater as an actor, and hosts a spirituality discussion on the Internet through www.ThirdAge.com.

Unconditional Love

By Claudia Mayorga

And in the end, it's not the years in your life that count. It's the life in your years.

Abraham Lincoln

John Mayorga was a fun-loving person who loved to laugh.

John was my husband of almost 30 years. We married young and grew up together. We loved each other unconditionally. As in all marriages, there were ups and downs; however, our love always carried us through. We had a full and happy life together, each of us with busy careers and our two terrific children. Angela and Carl were both out on their own; Angela was in medical school and Carl was working. Angela was truly a "daddy's girl," and Carl was much like John and respected him.

John was used to exercising every day. When he started getting winded very easily, he decided to see his doctor. Routine blood work was done. On Saturday, October 30, 1999, the call from John's doctor indicated that John's blood count was low and he should see a hematologist on Monday. One week later the diagnosis was confirmed: Hairy Cell Leukemia. This type of leukemia is recognized as one of the most treatable. The prognosis was excellent: a seven-day round of chemotherapy should take care of it.

On day six of the chemo, John was running a "fever of unknown origin" and was so ill that the doctor put him in the hospital. A week later he was released to continue recuperating at home. Although I continued going to work each day, it was really difficult leaving John alone. I remember coming home early one day and hearing him say he was thinking of calling me. He so appreciated everything I did for him.

The next two weeks were difficult. John was still spiking a fever. He was not his usual carefree, easy-going self. He was short with me and, because he didn't feel well, was very grouchy.

On December 16, John went back into the hospital because of the persistent fever. On December 22, the doctors determined that his spleen should be removed. It was hard to sit in the surgery waiting room. The surgeon came out after the operation and said they found a surprise: John had a gangrenous gallbladder. Every time he ate, his body was spewing infection. He continued running a fever and being pumped full of antibiotics. On December 30, John convinced the doctor to let him go home.

Our belated Christmas celebration was amazing. John was tired, but he forced himself to sit through opening gifts with the children he loved so much. Angela was scheduled to leave the next morning to go back to Omaha for a New Year's Eve celebration.

We had a quiet New Year's Day. On January 2, John began having trouble breathing. I called the doctor who suggested that we go to the hospital.

The pulmonologist placed him in ICU. I stayed for a while and then went home. During the night, John was put on a respirator. From that day forward, I was at the hospital each day to be with John.

ICU is not the most pleasant place to be. Days turned into weeks. Most days, I went to the hospital before going to work and returned in the late afternoon. I stayed until they closed ICU from 6:00 to 7:00 p.m. for the shift change and then came back after dinner. I was usually home by 9:30 each evening.

John's condition continued to deteriorate as one infection after another took hold. He was sedated and continued on the respirator.

During the second week of February, John was diagnosed with Vancomiacin Resistant Infection. I had to wear a gown and gloves when I was in his room. This was one of the most difficult times for me. It was another point at which I had to admit that things weren't going well.

On February 11, Angela came into town. When she walked into John's room, she commented about how much weight he'd lost. She met with the doctors while I was at home resting. When she left to go back to school on Sunday, she said she had to get things done so she could come back. I knew that meant things were not good. On Sunday evening, I told John that I knew how hard he'd fought and that if he couldn't fight any more, I'd understand.

On Valentine's Day, I went to the hospital that morning as usual. For some reason, I just couldn't leave John to go to work, so we spent the entire day together. John had always sent me flowers on Valentine's Day. That day, a dozen long-stemmed red roses were delivered to my office. Carl had sent them since John couldn't.

The next morning, I stopped by the hospital before going to work. I had a heavy interview schedule that day and needed to be at the office. Carl and I had planned to meet at the hospital at 5 p.m. I was running late. A few minutes after 5, I called Carl and asked where he was. He said he was at the hospital with a nurse who wouldn't let him go to John's room. He handed his phone to her and she told me that Dr. Hill was with John and things weren't looking good.

I immediately left the office for the 10-minute drive to the hospital. Dr. Hill came to see me and told me that all of John's functions were shutting down and they were performing CPR. He didn't see much hope for John's survival.

John had fought so hard! I told Dr. Hill that the kindest thing we could do was to let him go. Dr. Hill was wonderful. He let me cry on his shoulder. A few minutes later, the minister from our church arrived. John was pronounced dead shortly thereafter.

The next few days are a blur. There were funeral arrangements to make and family coming to town. All seven of my brothers came to support me. The blur continued for the next week and a half as I wrote thank you notes and prepared to return to work.

For about six-months, I cried at the drop of a hat. I was so devastated by this loss. Carl moved back home to be with me. He felt I shouldn't be alone.

I know I'll never stop missing John; however, life goes on and so shall I. Both Angela and Carl are married now. There was a white rose on the altar at both weddings to symbolize John's presence. We knew he was there with us.

After three years, I began to look for opportunities to date. Being 50 and single after almost 30 years of marriage is overwhelming. I persevered and am building a new life.

There are so many lessons I've learned from this experience. I've listed some of them here, in no particular order:

- Our loved ones are simply "on loan" from God.

- Life is short and you never know what's around the corner.

- Love like there's no tomorrow.

- Become self-sufficient in those matters you've not handled before.

- Rely on your inner strength ... there's more there than most people give themselves credit for.

- Change your approach to life. (I seldom get upset with situations. If I can change the situation, I will. If there's nothing I can do, I simply let it go. Life is too short to sweat the small stuff.)

- Use your experiences to help others through tough times.

- Be true to yourself and your values.

- Focus on the positive things in your life.

- Be open to the possibility of loving again.

21

I believe that the biggest lesson I've learned is to thank God every day for the many blessings He's bestowed. It's about being thankful for the time John and I had, for our loving family and for the wonderful memories I have to cherish and share with Angela and Carl.

Claudia Mayorga is a busy executive who enjoys spending her free time with her children and friends, playing golf, and reading the latest novels. She is also active in her local church. Having grown up in a family of nine children, she understands hard work and the concept of sharing.

Deafening Silence

By Dorothy Ostenfeld

There are as many nights as days, and the one is just as long as the other in the year's course. Even a happy life cannot be without a measure of darkness, and the word 'happy' would lose its meaning if it were not balanced by sadness.

Carl Jung

Silence … it's the first thing that really struck me as I held my husband's hand and he stopped breathing. That horrible gasping, rattling sound just stopped. I never realized silence could be so overwhelming.

Moe suffered from lung cancer for four years before he died. We had been married 30 years. With assistance from hospice, I was able to care for him until he died peacefully at home.

Soon, the family, the priest, and friends were there—all wanting to say goodbye before the undertaker arrived. I snapped back to reality when someone asked, "Can you make some coffee? Everyone could use a little something." For the next few days, I took care of a house full of people. That was the first step into my future: I was a grief-stricken widow, and still the caretaker.

Then the in-laws came—they cried and I consoled as I listened to the stories about their son and brother. I never heard from them again after the funeral. Thank God for our children; they really did help. Of course, they wondered whether they were left anything in the will! In our family, we manage to find a laugh in every situation, no matter how deep we have to look.

After the funeral, the really hard part began. All the simple, everyday things that needed to be taken care of … paying bills, cutting the grass, buying groceries for one. The first trip to the grocery store was a shock … buying what I liked instead of what he liked. What the heck did I like? It had been so long, I could hardly remember. Until now, everything had revolved around my husband … what to eat, what TV shows to watch, where to go, what to do.

It was hard emptying out his sick room, returning all the hospital equipment, cleaning out his clothes and personal things. I found things I didn't know he had kept—pictures and letters we had written to each other years ago. I cried a lot, but I made myself keep going, doing what had to be done.

The house that always seemed too small with the five of us in it suddenly seemed so large … too big for just one person. Our two kids had grown up and moved out a few years earlier; my mother, who had lived with us the last ten years of her life had recently died, and now Moe was gone, too. Taking one day at a time was all I could do. I kept busy during the day, but the evenings … evenings were the worst. There was too much time to think. I missed having someone to talk to about my day, about what was going on in the world, about family matters. I had no one to laugh with. God, quiet can be so loud!

People, especially friends, are very strange: while my husband was alive, we were a couple, invited to all the gatherings. We shared birthdays and holidays with our friends. We watched each other's children grow. We were part of the group. Then he got sick. At first, they rallied around, helping where and when they could. And we were grateful. But when the sickness dragged on, they slowly disappeared. I think people are uncomfortable when a patient lingers too long; they're afraid of saying or doing the wrong thing, so they just stop coming around.

Don't be surprised if you no longer hear from friends like these once you are a widow. Sure, they're busy; you're busy, too. But it's as if you're an extra shoe. You're no longer invited to things you were invited to as a couple. The same thing happened to my mother when my father died. Bless her soul; I didn't think too much about it back then, but now I know how she felt.

I think the best thing that happened to me was having very little money. That may sound strange, but it forced me to get up and get moving. I hadn't worked in years. What would I do? I did the only thing I could think of; I started babysitting in my home, taking care of three babies from 6 a.m. until 7 p.m. My days were full. This really helped me get through that long mourning period, as I settled into a routine: work, sleep and work again.

At some point, I began having a strange, recurring dream. I would get so angry I'd wake up shaking. In the dream, Moe had left me for another woman, and they had a baby together. We also had a baby, and I would be driving around with our baby in the car trying to find Moe. His mother (yes, she was in the dream, too) told me he no longer wanted me.

"But we're married," I said to her.

"Too bad; he wants to be with her," my mother-in-law responded.

I had this dream several times, and then suddenly it changed. In the new version, I had a knife, and I used it to stab him 17 times ... not 16, not 18 ... exactly 17 times. What in the world does that mean? I read a few dream books, but most of them refer to sweet, innocent dreams—nothing as savage as murder! And what's really disturbing is that I wake up smiling. It takes a few seconds to realize he really is dead, but I didn't kill him. It's been 10 years since he died, and I still have this crazy dream.

A few years after Moe died, I moved in with my daughter and son-in-law and their two sons. It was my son-in-law who insisted I move in with them; I wouldn't have considered it otherwise. I have a part-time job at a nursing home nearby, and I keep in touch with friends and family. Once again, my days are full.

I think the important thing to remember is that everyone is different. There is no one right way to mourn the death of a spouse. Everyone has to find their own way. Keeping busy and caring for others is the path I've chosen and one that seems to be working for me.

Dorothy Ostenfeld is a nursing home recreation assistant and lives in Pacific, MO with her daughter, son-in-law and two grandsons.

Death's Messenger

By Eva Bell

The English scientist Michael Faraday (1791-1867) is considered to have been one of the greatest experimental physicists. When Faraday was questioned on his speculations of a life after death, he replied: "Speculations? I know nothing about speculations. I'm resting on certainties. I know that my Redeemer lives, and because He lives, I shall live also."

It was December 30, 1968, and the smell of fruit cake baking in the oven wafted through the apartment. For the umpteenth time, my children and I peeked over the balcony at the sound of every car cruising by. We were expecting my husband, Jacob, who had been on duty over Christmas somewhere in South India. We had planned to make up for his Christmas absence by celebrating with a gala New Year's party.

And so, when a couple clad in black tapped on my door that evening, tragedy was furthest from my mind. Their long, morose faces made me wonder whether one of them was ill and had come for treatment. At that time, my consulting rooms were adjacent to my apartment. I showed them to their seats and was about to ask how I could be of help, when the woman, totally inexperienced in breaking bad news, began to spout poetry:

"Pale Death with impatient step knocks on the poor man's cottage and palaces of kings."

The man looked uncomfortably down at his hands.

"She must be suffering from depression," I thought.

Suddenly the woman jumped up and held me in a vice-like grip. "Don't hold back," she said. "Cry out as loud as you wish. Tears are cathartic. Let them flow."

"What are you talking about?" I asked, convinced that she was as nutty as my fruit cake. It still hadn't dawned on me that she was the bearer of bad tidings.

"Your husband is dead. His aircraft crashed this afternoon at a place called Ambasamudram. He died on the spot."

Now it was my turn to stare.

"You must be joking. Jacob is on his way home. He'll drive up any moment now."

"You're in shock," she insisted. "It's good if you can cry."

With that, these apparitions in black got up and marched out the door. They had done their duty. Though I've never set eyes on them again, I have often thought about the unfeeling, impersonal way the news of my husband's death was relayed to me.

Then I recalled something Jacob had mentioned a few months earlier, in connection with another pilot's death. He spoke of the "ravens in black" that had descended on the bereaved family to heartlessly inform them of their loss. The man was obviously the Personnel Manager of the company Jacob worked for and had come in the line of duty.

I sat there too stunned to move, my eight-year-old daughter and three-year-old son wondering why I had suddenly turned to stone. Before long, my eldest sister and her husband, who was also a pilot, came rushing in with more details of the accident. My sister had her own prescription for bereavement:

"No crying," she warned. "There's no need to make a public display of your grief."

I recalled what she had told me before my marriage. By then she had already been a pilot's wife for many years.

"You've got to have nerves of steel. Every time he leaves home, you'll wonder if he'll ever come back."

And so, I allowed not a sniffle to escape me until the lights were turned out at night and I could bury my face in my pillow and weep my heart out for the part of me that had died; for one so young and full of life; for a loving, caring individual with whom I had shared so many good times, in our short married life of nine-and-a-half years.

As a doctor, death is a familiar figure to me. It doesn't frighten me, but merely leaves a deep sadness that no matter what the status of a person, a life on earth has ended. When it comes unexpectedly to one of your own, however, it takes a while to sink in.

It didn't help that I had to wait for two long days for the body to be brought home to Bombay. The postmortem and various other formalities had to be completed. The body had to be brought by road to Madras, and then flown to Bombay. Those were incredibly long hours, filled with shock and denial.

"No, it can't be happening to me. There must be some mistake."

These thoughts kept going through my mind, even as relatives and friends thronged the house to console me. The finality of his death was only brought home when I saw him laid out in his coffin. His face was peaceful, and I knew for certain that he had gone home to be with his Lord.

The funeral took place at 9 p.m. on January 1, 1969. He was just 33 years old. It was a beautiful service that brought comfort to my heart. Jacob had crossed over from death to life because Jesus Christ had destroyed death and brought life and immortality to all who believe in Him. I can truly say that at no time did I feel any bitterness or anger. If God had taken my husband at such an early age, I knew that He had a definite plan for my life. I had to find out what it was. I was just thirty-two and the road ahead would be long and torturous.

When we had married in September, 1958, my husband was in the Indian Air Force. Transfers were fairly routine. Being a gynecologist, I always managed to get a job with accommodation, even when he was posted to non-family stations. But my career was not really my priority.

In 1965, my husband's contract with the Air Force was over and he opted for a lucrative job with a private company. He was a helicopter pilot and the company did crop dusting. He was out of station for at least two weeks each month, mostly in remote parts of the country.

As our son was very young, I didn't want to leave him with a nanny for long stretches of time, so I decided to open a clinic adjacent to my flat. Private practice was really not my cup of tea. My squeamishness about charging fees proved a disadvantage, and though I had many patients, the clinic was heavily subsidized by my husband.

So what was uppermost in my mind now that Jacob was gone was finding a job. I needed a steady income to support my little family. Having a profession was an advantage. I could have found a remunerative opening right there in Bombay. But my mother, who was visiting, realized I was being pulled in different directions by my elder siblings, my in-laws and friends. They were all so sure they knew what was best for me. I was very vulnerable. My husband had pampered me to such an extent that I didn't even know how to write a check, where to pay the bills, or where to buy groceries. Now each of these loved ones was ready to overwhelm me with their concern.

"It would be best to relocate," Mother counseled. "You must discover your own strengths, make your own decisions and stand firmly on your own two feet. Allowing yourself to be cosseted will make you less inclined to do things for yourself. Don't let anyone pity or patronize you."

How thankful I was for that advice. Besides, the air field from which my husband used to fly was so close to the apartment that helicopters flying overhead throughout the day brought back many memories and increased the gnawing ache in my heart. I had to get away. I could not afford to sink into depression or languish in self-pity. Jacob would never have approved of that.

A large Mission hospital in the South needed a gynecologist. Much to the chagrin of my sisters and despite their grim predictions, I moved out from Bombay overnight with my family.

Mission hospital work is always very busy and my specialty is a round-the-clock job. I was accommodated in a large bungalow with a high-tiled roof and cavernous rooms, and too many windows. At night it felt eerie. Bats flapped around in the attic, and wild cats raced along the rafters. My children and I huddled together in one room until we got bolder. My city-bred children took time to settle into this rural milieu. My mother offered to stay with us and tended to the house, the maids and the children, leaving me free to throw myself into my work.

Work saved me from self-pity. I had no time to brood. But it also made me distance myself from my children. I knew they were being well-cared for by my mother. She made up for my indifference, allowing me to work through my own private grief. When I had time, I began writing a novel about a wartime romance, and a girl who passed off someone's baby as her own in the hope of saving her marriage.

Even with my writing, it was a time of loneliness. Not even my children could enter into this private pain of bereavement. The marital bond uniting two people into one flesh was gone. Beside me at night was the vacant space that greeted me each time I slipped into bed. There was no one to cling to, no one to confide in. I felt like an amputee; the pain in the phantom limb often made me cry out in desperation. I had a great deal of fear, too. How would I cope alone with two young children? It's all very well to say, "The Lord sustains the fatherless and the widow."

But my work and my writing proved therapeutic. I needed neither medication nor counseling. I had a deep assurance that I was never going to be alone. There was a purpose for my life and in His own good time, God would reveal it to me. Before that, however, I had to be "tried in the furnace of affliction."

Exactly a year after I took this job, Mother lay on her bed one morning and never woke up. I felt desolate. Now my children and I were all alone. We had lost two people in the course of one year. I couldn't continue with this job as it was too demanding, and I wouldn't have any time for my children.

I moved to Mangalore 60 miles away where I had spent my childhood, and took a job that didn't involve night duties. But I was nervous about living alone in a city. People were under the impression that I had inherited a lot of money from my husband. Suddenly, I discovered I had many relatives. There were loan-seekers, confidence-tricksters, mischief-makers and lechers. My stress levels soared as I tried to keep them all at bay. My children were becoming very insecure.

There was one cousin who helped me with my legal problems. He also helped me in many small ways and tried to instill in me courage to cope. But within a few months, he died of a massive heart attack. One by one, my props were crumbling. There was no one to rely on. I felt emotionally and physically drained.

Now there was only one Person who could give me comfort and safety. He wanted my total commitment in exchange for His protection and love. I received this assurance:

> *Do not be afraid—you will not suffer shame;*
> *Do not fear disgrace—you will not be humiliated;*

...You will remember no more the reproach
of your widowhood,
For your Maker is your husband.

Isaiah 54: 1-5

That was when I finally felt ready to face the world. The memory of Jacob would always be an integral part of my life, but now there was work for me to do. At last, I could see the light at the end of the tunnel.

Incredible advances were being made in the world of medicine and I did not want to be left behind. In September 1972, I went to the U.K. for postgraduate work in gynecology and obstetrics. My children were admitted to a boarding school in Mangalore, where the nuns took good care of them. Once again, this was a challenge. I was going back to academics after an interval of 14 years. But those were wonderful years. Hard work and intense study got me my degree. Besides, in England, I never felt alienated because of my single status, whereas, in India, social life was severely restricted. As widows were synonymous with bad luck, I was excluded from all auspicious occasions. A widow's movements were perpetually under scrutiny, and wagging tongues could tear her reputation to shreds for imagined transgressions.

Since then, I've traveled widely and worked in different parts of the world. But my calling was back home. I served the same Mission hospital to which I had fled soon after my bereavement for 17 long years. I was Director and Obstetrician/Gynecologist. It became one of the best known institutions in that part of the country, catering to the needs of thousands of poor and underprivileged people. I was also able to obtain a degree in Theology, and indulge in my first love—writing. This was the purpose that God had in mind for me.

Today, I am retired from hospital work, but spend my time as a freelance writer. Women's issues are my special interest. I also spend time counseling women and girls on various issues. Widowhood has made me sensitive to the pain of others.

To the newly bereaved, I would like to say:

- Don't be afraid to grieve. Keeping a stiff upper lip is an invitation to prolonged pain, introversion, despair and psychosomatic illnesses.

- There is a time to weep and a time to recover. The sooner one learns to let go, the quicker the period of healing.

- Reinterpret your situation in a positive light. Enumerate your skills and resources and make them work for you.

- Refuse to be pitied or patronized.

- Motivate yourself to be self-confident. "The mind needs the scaffolding of self-confidence that enables one to adjust to new situations," says Dr. Amelia McCool.

- Find a few friends who are good listeners.

- Feel free to reinvest in love if you are so inclined, but do not do so on the rebound. Give yourself time to recover. One need have no guilt on this score. The marriage commitment ends with the death of one partner.

- Seek fellowship with God. Faith provides resources to deal with grief. There is no point in questioning God's motives. Perfect trust will lead you to the light at the end of the tunnel.

- Remember: "Out of the presses of pain comes the soul's best wine and the eyes that have shed no rain, can shed but little shine." (A.B. Simpson)

Eva Bell is a gynecologist/obstetrician and has been a freelance writer for many years. In addition to writing short stories for adults and children, she has also published articles in newspapers, magazines and anthologies in India, as well as on websites. She has two novels to her credit: Silver Amulet (1998) and When Shadows Flee (2001). Eva Bell has also written a children's book, Lost on the Beach (1970) and a nonfiction book, Grace Abounding (1986).

MY JOSIE

By Ronn Venable

(Seen on a headstone in a cemetery in Ireland): Death leaves a heartache no one can heal; Love leaves a memory no one can steal.

I remember the first time I saw Josie: she was 16 and sitting on the neo-gothic steps of our midwestern hometown courthouse with some friends. She threw her head back with a laugh, and the sunset-orange of her long, frizzy hair framed her face, accenting deep green eyes that looked right through me as we gazed at each other. In her hip-hugging, bell-bottom denims, she was a 17-year-old boy's rock 'n roll fantasy girl, a freckled cross between Janis Joplin and Stevie Nicks.

I think I knew then that she was "the one," but as we grew older, we stopped dating and drifted apart. For almost 20 years we didn't see each other; she had married and moved to Oklahoma and I had read Jack Kerouac's *On the Road* and discovered a wanderlust that kept me traveling the United States for a number of years, avoiding long-term relationships and dodging commitment.

Then, in 1981, a week before my 30th birthday, I was involved in a serious automobile accident that left me hospitalized for six months, a thousand miles from home. I wrote to old friends to pass the time and one of them suggested I contact Josie. She was back in our hometown, single once more. My friend had known me long enough to know my history with Josie and that I had pined for her most of my life.

The Internet hadn't happened yet, and all of our contact was via snail mail. I wrote her long, flowing letters about my life, my philosophy and my desires. Soon, we made arrangements to meet; I would fly back home and we would finally see each other again. On crutches, I hobbled through airports and baggage checks, making my way to my destiny.

When I first saw her again, I think I fell in love immediately. In my eyes, she hadn't changed from the petite teenager I met all those years ago. With the sun haloing her still-frizzy hair, her beauty captured me; once again, I couldn't take my eyes off her.

I was surprised when, after just six months of letters and phone calls, she readily agreed to move her family to Florida so we could be together. Her faith in life and in me, along with her sense of adventure, enamored me. We rented a house and, with her two pre-teen sons, she and I began to get to know each other better. We were married within the year. At the time, I was 32, she was 30, we were happy, and I was certain I had made the best decision of my life. That was 1982, and the years that followed were my happiest as Josie, the son she gave me, and my two stepsons became my life.

October 4, 1999 began like any other day ... the commute to work was the same as always: too few lanes for too many cars. The sun was beginning to crest the horizon and the deep blue sky was marbled with wisps of ever-changing white as I drove to work. I couldn't know that within a few hours, my world would be turned upside down. At the moment, I was as happy as I could ever hope to be. Everything was perfect.

Continuing my routine, I arrived at work, turned on lights, started coffee, shuffled papers and called home to wake Josie. I looked forward to calling her each morning and hearing her soft voice, giving me another opportunity to tell her I loved her. My first call went unanswered. I chuckled to myself; she was known to turn the ringer off if she didn't need to get up early. It was 8:30 a.m. I would try again later.

At 11 a.m., I still hadn't been able to reach her, and I was disappointed that she may have gone out, missing my calls. Maybe I could catch her later ...

At 11:15 a.m., the intercom chirped and I was informed that I had a call on line one. "Must be her," I told myself as I made my way to the phone. But it wasn't. It was my son Ron. The words he spoke chilled me to the core: "Dad, you'd better get home ... I think Mom is dead." My face flushed and I felt light-headed; was this some sort of horrific dream? I dropped what I was doing and headed out the door. My car was moving before I was settled in the seat and I kept saying over and over, "Don't let this be true. Please, God, don't let this be true." A mile down the road, I pulled up to a pay phone; maybe I misunderstood Ron. Maybe he was wrong. Maybe this <u>was</u> a dream. As I dialed the number, I asked God to let any one of those be true.

Ron answered the phone, and then a paramedic immediately came on the line. It was true: Josie had died sometime that morning, her heart beating its last while she slept. Later we would learn that she had died from a heart attack. There was no warning; one minute she was alive and the next she wasn't. As I drove the 15 miles home, tears blurred my vision, and I continued to repeat aloud, "Don't let this be true, don't let this be true; don't let this be true." The worst day of my life had begun.

I turned onto our street and saw the red and blue lights of the police car, fire truck and ambulance in front of our home. Soon, I knew I was going to have to admit the truth and be slapped in the face by reality. As I approached the driveway, I saw the coroner's van coming down the street. My heart sank deeper into my chest.

That afternoon after everyone had left, my sons and I tried to make sense of what had happened. We looked at each other, unable to speak, confused and sickened with grief. The thought struck me that suddenly I was <u>the</u> parent now. Josie was no longer there to help me. I wasn't ready for this; Josie had always taken care of the day-to-day parenting duties. Slowly, I admitted to myself that I wasn't sure I knew how to be a strong parent. I wasn't even sure I could be strong for myself. I always prided myself on being a realist, but this reality was far beyond what I wanted to acknowledge.

Devastation was all I knew that day and for several days after. Everything in our home reminded me of her and how much I was going to miss her. Imagining my life without her at my side was impossible. I pictured myself as a lonely, bitter old man, looking forward to the day I would die and leave the pain behind. Each night when I lay down in our bed alone, or had an exciting epiphany I wanted to share with Josie, I was reminded that this was not a dream.

I was angry that she had left me. Why did this have to happen? Why did my sons have to suffer so much pain at such young ages? I wanted to lash out at anyone who happened to get in my way. My driving became more aggressive and my usually irreverent, cavalier attitude about nearly everything became much more serious. The pain of each waking moment ate at my soul, but I couldn't give up; I had to survive for the sake of our sons.

The night that Josie died, I sat in front of the computer, trying to occupy my mind and ease the pain I was feeling. I emailed my sister on Guam, telling her of my loss. She was the big sister I had turned to my entire life, ready as always to comfort with her wisdom and support.

I had never visited chat rooms before. That night, however, I found an online grief support group. I emptied my heart to the two participants in the chat room, and as we "talked," I began to feel some relief. The act of putting my pain into words seemed to calm me. We chatted for an hour, and when I signed off, I was able to sleep, resting my eyes, my mind and my heart.

The chat room proved to be my salvation. Miriam, a woman I met there, was especially supportive. We began communicating daily, and she let me talk for hours of my love for Josie. Miriam encouraged me to look for comfort within myself and to have the faith that I could survive and be a good father.

Coming to grips with my wife's sudden passing was further complicated when, just two days later, I learned that my own health was in jeopardy. Tests confirmed the reason my blood had been rejected when I recently attempted to donate: I had Hepatitis C. Now my attention was diverted to my own survival and the well-being of our sons. I had to devote my time and attention to running our household—something I'd never had to deal with before. I had to push my emotions aside and focus on paying bills, fixing dinner and staying alive.

Since Josie's death, I've had a couple of dreams about her. The first was on the first night I was alone. As I slept, I found myself in a meadow with a path winding its way to me. Josie was walking that path toward me, with Jesus and her father at her side. As they drew closer, I was elated to see her and was overcome with a feeling of joy. I got down on my knees and begged Jesus to let her come back to me, but he gently touched my shoulder and told me he needed her with him. In a voice as soft as silk but with the authority of thunder, he told me that each time I looked at a sunset and saw the purple hues of light (purple was Josie's favorite color) as the sun sank to the horizon and the sky darkened, I could be assured that Josie was watching over us. Somehow, that comforted me. To this day, I find myself looking at sunsets and hoping for a purple hue. Some days I laugh out loud when a purple sky appears as the sun sets.

The second dream left me with a profound sense of loss. In the dream, Josie walked into the room with a presence that overwhelmed me. I felt tremendous relief when I saw her. I didn't ask her where she had been; I simply hugged her and told her how glad I was that she was back. Her green eyes pierced my soul as she told me she couldn't stay. She told me she loved me and our sons and she was glad I was with them. She also said she knew I could make it. Her words echoed in my ears, and I recalled long-gone days when I would be questioning myself, and Jodie would look at me and say, "You can do it, Ronn; You can do anything you want." The dream ended when she kissed me gently and quietly left the room. The sorrow I felt was as deep and penetrating as that of my first few days without her.

There isn't a day that goes by when I don't think about my wife, lover and best friend, but I am trying to move on. Not long after Josie died, the boys and I started planning for our own future, trying hard to look beyond our loss. Having spent my life wishing I had time to become a writer, I adopted the motto, "Carpe Diem" and enrolled in a creative writing class at the local community college. The class became my motivation and distraction, both from my grief and my own illness.

In the years since Josie died, Miriam and I have seen each other a few times and we continue to communicate daily. She has been there for me unconditionally and continues to listen to me when I speak of my love for Josie as attentively as when I talk of my fondness for her. My desire to love again has been satisfied by this wonderful woman who understands my plight and offers compassion as well as passion and the possibility of a future together.

As I recount this, I realize I'm not sure I have ever dealt with my loss completely. I don't believe I've had closure. Although I grieved for Josie, and our family revered her with a heartfelt memorial service, all the while I had to think of my own survival and how important it had become for my children. Since losing her, I've never stopped long enough to reflect on our life together, nor have I observed my loss as anything more than another challenge to deal with. At times, I feel guilty for the clinical approach I've taken; other times I wish I cold go back to the day she died and cancel my doctor's appointment so that I'd never learn about my own health problems and could instead focus my attention on the wounds that scar my heart.

Someday, I hope to be able to clear my head of all thoughts of my own survival and focus on how much I loved Josie, how important we were to each other and how well we worked together. Then, I would cry from deep within my soul and find that place where I can go and come to terms with all the passion and desire I'll never be able to express to her, to take the hurt that fills my days and transform it into an antiseptic to heal my broken heart.

After Josie's death and becoming aware of his own mortality, Ronn Venable has pursued his childhood dream of becoming a writer. Since then, he has published numerous short stories, essays and articles. He lives in the Ohio Valley near his two sons.

LIFE WITHOUT LARRY

By Julie Raque

Unable are the Loved to die, For Love is Immortality.

Emily Dickinson

The alarm went off at 5:15 a.m., as it did every weekday morning. Larry got up and headed for the showers. Once he was out, I took my turn. We both proceeded to get ready for work, talking quietly so as not to wake our children, 7 month-old Chelsea and 2-1/2 year-old Patrick. This was our typical morning. There was no reason for either of us to suspect that this would be the last morning of our life together.

When Larry left for work at 5:55 a.m., I noticed that it was raining steadily, but didn't give it any more thought. An hour and a half later, I received a call from the police department telling me that my husband had been involved in an accident and that I should get to the local hospital immediately. I later learned that Larry had sustained severe head trauma in a head-on collision. The accident had occurred when the other driver, whose vision had been obscured in the downpour, became confused and inadvertently ended up going the wrong direction on the highway.

Larry died the next day without regaining consciousness. At the hospital and for the next several days I was surrounded by our family, friends, coworkers and neighbors. But soon they went back to their own lives, and I was left to deal with mine … a life I never expected and certainly didn't want.

The experts define "denial," the first stage of the grieving process, as the "No, not me!" stage. This certainly defined my reaction. I kept saying, "No! Not Larry!" I couldn't believe he was actually dead. If you had asked those who knew him whether they thought Larry would live a long life, they would undoubtedly have answered, "Yes!" He was a strong man. He had strong values; his priorities were in order, and he was determined to fulfill his roles as husband and father.

When he committed to anything—a purpose or a person—he committed completely.

That's why I couldn't accept the fact that my husband was dead. Larry had made a commitment to me and our children, and I knew that, given the choice, he would never abandon us. While I've always had a strong faith, I couldn't understand why God would take a young husband and father. How could I be expected to raise our two kids alone? Larry was the better parent, the better person. How could God let this happen?

At the same time that denial had me in its clutches, anger was running a close second. Mostly I was angry at the other driver ... angry at his stupidity, his lack of judgment, his insane actions. The fact that I never got a chance to actually see him may very well have been a blessing in disguise.

I was also angry at God. I was angry that he had denied Larry the joy of raising his kids. I was angry that God had chosen me to be a single parent. How did he expect me to support my children alone? God knew that Larry had been the main provider. The load I was forced to bear pushed me right past the bargaining stage into the fourth stage of grief—depression.

In the weeks following Larry's death, I tried to focus on the immediate needs of the children and returning to my job. It wasn't long before I suffered from headaches from the time I woke up until the time I fell into bed, exhausted, at the end of the day. I took Tylenol every four hours. When the alarm went off in the morning, I would just lie there, hitting the snooze button again and again. I felt as though I could sleep forever.

I remember my close friend, Pam, calling to check on me. She asked me how I was sleeping and told me not to be afraid to ask the doctor for something to help me sleep if I needed to. I remember thinking that something must be seriously wrong with me: I should be having trouble sleeping, when in fact, that's all I wanted to do! I started feeling guilty about being able to sleep. "I must not be grieving enough," I thought.

About a week later, one of my bosses gave me a brochure about depression. The symptoms included "not sleeping/sleeping too much." Now I felt better, knowing that I wasn't "abnormal," and that my desire to sleep was just my way of dealing with grief.

For the next several months, I bounced from denial to anger to depression and back again. One day the depression would be at its worst; the next day I'd be struggling with the pain of shock and anger.

In the beginning, there were many mornings when I would awaken and desperately want to just lie there. But then one of the kids would wake up and I would be forced to get out of bed and do what needed to be done. I focused on getting through just two or three hours at a time: breakfast; put the kids on the floor to play, plop myself down on the couch; 11:30 a.m.—lunchtime; after lunch, naptime for all of us (although Patrick didn't always sleep, he was willing to watch videos while I napped on the couch); following naps—snacktime; play time; dinner time; bath time; bed time. And tomorrow I'd get to do it all over again.

The worst part was not having anyone to share the duties with; I had no one to talk to while the kids played, no one I could turn to when I needed a break. This is when it hit me like a slap in the face—I was truly alone.

Months passed, and winter turned into spring. As part of my spring cleaning routine, I decided it was time to clean out Larry's closet and drawers. I put everything in boxes, took them down to the basement and shoved them into a corner.

Not long after, I had a dream that Larry was back; it was the weekend and we were together as usual. I was on the floor playing with Patrick and Larry walked in and said he was going to get dressed. He left the room and returned a few minutes later, asking where all his things were. I answered, "Oh, I must have packed everything up and put them downstairs." Both of us just stood there and looked at each other, not saying another word. That's when the dream ended.

Did that dream have a special meaning? Maybe I was feeling guilty about moving his things out of our room. Or maybe it was just Larry's way of letting me know he was still around me and our children, still part of our family. This was the first of many dreams about Larry that would eventually lead me to believe that he is our Guardian Angel.

About a year after Larry's death, a friend asked me how I was doing and if I felt I was moving forward. I told her that I didn't think I was quite there yet. "I'm not done dealing with all this. I know that, because at the end of the day, I have nothing left. All energy sources are completely drained and borderline bankrupt. I know I'll be able to say 'I'm fine,' when the day comes that at bedtime I have energy left over." For me, that was around the two-year mark, and I believe it was a gradual awakening and realization that I was going to survive.

If I were going to offer advice to someone whose spouse has died, I would tell them to "STOP! STOP EVERYTHING! Take some time off work. Get a handle on the daily chores. Simplify your life as much as possible. Merge all bank accounts into just one or two. Clean out the house; organize things. Your life has been turned upside down. The first thing you need to do is take time to realize what has happened. The 'normal' you once knew is gone. Now you must slowly adjust to a new 'normal.'"

*"From Surviving to Thriving: Young Widowhood With Kids"
– this is the story of how, Julie Raque at the age of 29, woke up
at the usual 5:15 AM a happily married woman and mother
of an infant and a toddler and within two hours was widowed.
As her story continues, and it does, you'll struggle with Julie
for six years as she learns the hard lessons that pull her and
her two children through the grief process and rebuilds their
lives in a way she never thought possible without her husband.*
http://www.matrixcoachingservices.com

Dear Jon

By Laurel Sparks

*I believe that imagination is stronger than
knowledge — myth is more potent than history
— dreams are more powerful than facts — hope
always triumphs over experience — laughter is
the cure for grief — love is stronger than death.*

Robert Fulghum

On one of my aunt and uncle's visits to Indiana
about ten years ago, I was suffering from the breakup of
a stormy relationship that my partner ended. My Aunt
Wanda (by marriage), ever the matchmaker, wanted to
help me and suggested I write to a nephew of hers who
lived in Alaska. Devastated as I was at the time, I said I
would think about it.

Little did I know how this man in Alaska would eventually change my life.

Aunt Wanda mentioned a few things about Jon, believing that he and I had things in common. We were near the same age, he was career-oriented, as was I. Half listening to what she was saying, I assumed she was only trying to cheer me up.

Aunt Wanda asked my permission to give Jon my address. I agreed, never thinking about the consequences, and never for a minute thinking anything positive would come of it.

Much to my surprise, the first letter from this stranger arrived within weeks of my aunt and uncle's departure. Jon described himself, his likes and dislikes, job and hobbies, and his surroundings in Alaska. I read the letter with interest, but put it away for future reference.

I was still distraught about my recent breakup.

The next letter arrived several weeks later. I had not yet replied to Jon's first one. This time he talked about what attracted him to women. He also told me that he had spent time in the Navy in the Vietnam era, and expressed some of his aspirations and goals.

By this time, I was becoming curious. Before I could get a letter off to him, he called. We talked as if we had known each other all our lives. At the end of our conversation, he invited me to Alaska for a visit. Even though I was enthusiastic, I was also hesitant. Things were moving way too fast.

In a strange way, and in a very short time, Jon made me feel worthwhile and strong again. He had a way of making me feel special and complete, even from thousands of miles away. I hadn't felt this way in a long time.

We began learning more about each other through more frequent letters and phone calls. Aunt Wanda was right; we did have the same interests. I found myself rushing home from work each day, hoping for a letter from Jon.

Within two months time, Jon had accepted a position in Denver and made plans to move there. Now we would at least be physically closer, so the chances of a relationship seemed more realistic.

The end of that year was approaching, so feeling quite bold, I invited him to spend New Year's Eve with me. When he readily accepted, I nearly panicked!

Scared as I was to encounter him face to face, I would have to muster up the courage to take that next step.

Should I go through with this? Had I done the right thing in asking him? Letters and calls were one thing, meeting him was an entirely different situation. Was there any way to back out?

I felt like an acrobat tumbling in mid-air. Would this man be able to catch me before I hit the ground? Or would he let me go while I tried desperately to hang on?

I wasn't emotionally ready for a commitment, not even a small one. I didn't want to be hurt again. My relationship history was not one with bragging rights. A charter member of the heartbreak club, I had a habit of misjudging men. Was I continuing the same pattern with Jon?

Something deep down was telling me to take the chance. Jon's words leaped out at me from his pages, from his voice. I read his letters over and over and replayed our conversations in my mind, searching for some hidden meaning, for a solution to my peril in regards to relationships.

The big day arrived when I was to pick up Jon at the airport. I waited in the terminal and saw the plane approaching. This was it—there was no turning back!

As the passengers deplaned, I drew back into the crowd, not wanting him to see me just yet. I spotted him right away; his description of himself had been accurate. I didn't know why I was hesitant, but when I stepped forward, he recognized me immediately from the photos I had sent.

Nervous as I was, Jon made me feel comfortable from the start. We held hands, snuggled, couldn't get enough of each other. It was as if we had been together for years. His gentle actions reacquainted me with a passion I had buried deep within myself.

The holiday was short, but memorable. I introduced him to my family and friends, and they instantly took to him.

When it was time to part, the ride back to the airport was short and awkward. As we bid each other farewell, in a small way, I was relieved. The encounter was over. We departed with fond memories.

The next letter from Jon arrived within days of his visit. It contained the words I had hoped he would write. He had fallen in love over New Year's. The feeling was reciprocated, although I didn't confess as easily.

We both knew we had left a part of ourselves with one another.

The distance between us now seemed bigger than ever. The next few months were long and miserable. My arms were as empty as my nights. What were we to do?

Finally, he asked me to consider living in Denver. At this point, we both wanted our relationship to be more permanent. I didn't give him an answer right away, as I had strong roots in Indiana and it would be difficult to pack up and leave.

Before I could respond, much to my surprise, he left Denver and went back home to Alaska. He was presented with a career position he couldn't decline. Not only was I flabbergasted, but heartsick too. Once again, the distance between us grew.

After that, our letters ceased. Shockingly, he had been another heartache for me. I had reached out once again and trusted, only to be misled.

My life seemed as void as ever while I coped with the loss. Months passed without letters or phone calls. Once more, I managed to get on with my life.

In time, he begged me to forgive him and to try to understand his decision to return to his homeland where he was comfortable.

It was not easy to ignore his plea as I wanted so much to mend our relationship.

Eventually, we both forgave and forgot.

Before long, I had to admit to myself that I missed him and wanted more than telephone calls, gifts, and letters. Yet I still couldn't shed fragments from my past, including his decision to return to Alaska. When he left Denver, it was as if he had left me, just like the men from my past relationships. I quarreled with my feelings in spite of the fact that Jon was making every effort to build up not only my ego, but our relationship again.

As time went on, we discussed our future more than a few times. Soon, Jon and I decided we needed to be together, permanently. A long distance love affair was impossible, improbable.

Jon started making plans to move to Indiana. As the months dragged on before he would join me, we remained strong. I began counting the days, the hours, the minutes until his arrival.

Coming home from work one day, I saw an unfamiliar car in my driveway. A closer look revealed he had made it. Jon was standing at my front door. At that moment, I knew my future was intact, that we had both made the right decision.

Our reception was warm, enticing, almost mesmerizing.

The next few months were trying times as we made adjustments and changes. Each of us had led very independent lives, an aspect that was hard to overcome. But overcome we did.

Jon and I married the next New Year's Eve, the anniversary of our first face-to-face meeting, at our Uncle Don and Aunt Wanda's house in Virginia. It seemed only right to be married there, since they had started us on the road to destiny. The doubts, the fears, the loneliness we had separately experienced were put behind us.

Way behind us.

Two years and a few months after our marriage, Jon died of a brain aneurysm. A part of me died also. He held a place in my heart no one will ever be able to fill.

With help from a great support network of family and friends, and a few articles and books on recovery from the loss of a loved one, I gradually restored my spirit and will to live. But not without experiencing depression and denial for months on end.

Admittedly, I don't consider myself a religious believer in any one faith, yet I do trust there is a higher power. And I'm not sure if my belief has played a part in my fate, but never a day goes by without me envisioning Jon and talking to him before I go to sleep. He is my guardian angel and still an influential part of my life.

Unbeknownst to him, Jon reinvented me. With respect, compliments, support, love, and encouragement, he made me into the strong person I am today. No other man could compare, or ever will.

Strangely enough, there is a particular robin outside my living room window that just won't fly far from my home. Could it be Jon protecting me?

As I think back now, I often wondered if the experience with Jon had all been a dream, a fantasy, or a fairy tale.

Whether it was fate, luck, circumstance, or Aunt Wanda that brought us together, he was my "Dear Jon."

And I'll sincerely be his, forever, in my heart.

After Jon's departure, Laurel concentrated on her passion of writing. Not only does she support her love of the written word with a paying profession of radio commercial advertising, but she has a few publishing credits to her name. Laurel's short stories and poems can be read in ezines "The Sidewalk's End," "Long Story Short: A Woman's Writer's Showcase," "Apollo's Lyre," "Seven Seas Magazine," "The Cynic Online Magazine," and in print in the 2005 Winter Issue of "The SiNK: A Literary Journal Considering All Things."

Georgia's Goodbye

By Mike Smith

I wanted a perfect ending. Now I've learned, the hard way, that some poems don't rhyme, and some stories don't have a clear beginning, middle, and end. Life is about not knowing, having to change, taking the moment and making the best of it, without knowing what's going to happen next. Delicious Ambiguity.

Gilda Radner

In September, 2002 I moved from Ohio to New Jersey for my job. My wife, Georgia, and I had decided that she and our two children would stay back in Ohio for the school year. Our daughter was entering her last year of high school and had been accepted into a special program allowing her to study at the community

73

college every afternoon. We didn't want her to miss this opportunity.

I was aware that Georgia wasn't feeling well, but she had refused to see a doctor.

When I returned for Thanksgiving she still hadn't gone to a doctor and claimed she was all right. I knew she wasn't and encouraged her to see someone.

By Christmas, she still hadn't gone.

On my trip home for Valentine's Day in 2003, I made Georgia promise to see a doctor. She didn't look well and was hardly eating. She finally made the appointment and was diagnosed with cirrhosis of the liver. Years of alcohol abuse had taken its toll.

Georgia was put on medication and ordered not to drink anymore.

On my trip home for our 19th wedding anniversary in April, she was in the hospital. Her condition had deteriorated and her skin had that yellowish color that comes with liver disease. She was stabilized and released.

When I returned in June for our daughter's graduation, Georgia was hardly able to get around.

It was at this point I began to wonder if she would recover.

We scheduled moving her and our son to Jersey in mid-August. Two days before the scheduled date she was admitted to the hospital again. Her potassium levels had reached a dangerously high level, and there was concern her kidneys could be damaged.

She insisted our son and I continue with the move. She was only supposed to be in the hospital a few days. The movers came and went, and my son and I headed to Jersey. The few days turned into a month. Georgia's kidneys had failed. She was now in critical condition, with both liver and kidney failure.

The case worker called me in early September and said, "Mr. Smith, we are giving Mrs. Smith dialysis today, sending her to you tomorrow, and the next day you have to get her to the dialysis center in Jersey."

I arranged a plane ticket for Georgia, and because of her condition, they allowed her to sit in first class. When they brought her to me in a wheel chair, I couldn't believe my eyes. My lovely wife had aged 30 years, her legs and feet swollen into useless clubs.

We got her into the car and drove home. She was able to get out of the car and walk to the front steps, but wasn't able to climb them. She was too heavy to carry, but our son and I managed to get her to the top landing by lifting her legs for her. At the door she fell to her hands and knees. Our son, just 16 years old, got upset and ran to his room where I could hear him banging things around. Unable to get Georgia up by myself, I called 911 for assistance. They couldn't force her to go to the hospital, so they brought her inside and made her comfortable on the sofa.

When I talked to my son later he said to me, "Dad! What happened to her? That's not my mom down there!" There was nothing I could say to calm him. What can you say to a son who sees a strange woman, knows it's his mom, but is unable to comprehend the changes that have taken place?

The next day I had to call for assistance to get her into my car and to the dialysis center. Two policemen came and helped me get her to her feet and to the bathroom. I remember looking at them and apologizing for having to put them through this. They assured me it was OK, all part of the job and all. I knew they were uncomfortable. I looked at one of them, saw the look in his eye and said, "If I ever become like that, do me a favor, and take that gun you have, and blow my freakin' head off." He shook his head sadly, "I understand, Mr. Smith."

At the dialysis center, I was told she probably wouldn't live long. With two major organs failed, her chances of survival without a transplant were slim. Ambulance transportation was arranged to take her to and from the center three times a week.

As the days turned into weeks, Georgia grew weaker and weaker. Her life revolved around lying on the sofa with two or three trips to the bathroom each day. At first she managed with a walker. I would sit her up on the sofa, reach down, hug her under the arms, whisper, "I love you" and lift her to her feet. From there she could grab the walker and get to the bathroom.

Within two weeks she was so weak that she needed me to support her even with the walker.

I was working long hours in a stressful position during the day and nursing my wife through the nights. Our son was a wreck. It was hard for him to watch his mother deteriorate. I was even worse. My hands shook constantly. I remember one night when Georgia called me for help while I was cooking dinner. I put my face in my hands and cried, "How am I going to manage?" Georgia heard me and started crying. I felt terrible. How could I be so inconsiderate? My wife was dying and I was concerned about myself.

A few weeks later the poisons in her body caused her to hallucinate. One day I came in the door, and she was crying. I asked what was wrong. "I fell down!" she cried.

"Fell down? Honey, if you fell down, how did you get back on the sofa?"

"I fell off my horsie," she sobbed.

I called 911. She was admitted to the hospital and the next day was on life support.

A week later I made my usual call to the hospital and was informed that Georgia had a bad day. "Are you coming to visit tonight, Mr. Smith?"

I thought that was a dumb question. I visited every night. I would sit by her bed and tell her about my day and what the kids were up to. She was in an induced coma and acknowledged none of it.

"Of course I am." I told the nurse. Warning bells were going off in my head. Why did she ask such a question?

When I went to her room and sat by her bed, the nurse said, "The doctor needs to talk to you. There are decisions to be made. The doctor is busy right now but would appreciate if you could wait for him."

My heart sank. I assured her I would wait. I knew what was coming.

I sat there for 40 minutes waiting for the doctor. They were the worst 40 minutes of my life. I knew I was going to be asked to shut off life support. I sat, then paced, then sat again. All the time I was crying and talking to my Georgia: "Honey, the doctor wants to see me. I know what it is. They are going to want my permission to turn off life support." Georgia and I had discussed this a long time ago and decided we would never let the other live on life support if there was no hope of recovery. "Honey, I know what I have to do and pray you understand and will forgive me."

I was a mess. I was crying, praying and pacing. I had just recently moved to the Fort Lee area of New Jersey and the only friends I had were co-workers and a few people I knew at the gym. All my family, a mother and two brothers, lived in back in Canada. I felt more alone than I have ever felt in my life.

The doctor finally came in, put a hand on my shoulder and told me the news. "There is a time when we are prolonging life and there is a time when we are prolonging death. There is nothing more we can do for your wife. We feel it would be best to take life support away and let nature takes its course." Through tears, I agreed.

My daughter flew in from Ohio. She hadn't seen her mom for a month and couldn't believe her eyes. The doctors left us alone for a few moments to say good-bye.

We left the room while they removed the machines and tubes. I was glad to have my daughter with me. My son refused to come. We returned to the room and sat on each side of Georgia's bed where we could each hold one of her hands. She was breathing in gasps. She was in a natural coma now, the drugs no longer needed. We held her hands, prayed, and even managed to crack a few jokes.

After about 20 minutes, Georgia's breathing paused for a few seconds and then resumed. As the minutes passed the pauses became more frequent and lasted longer. My daughter and I watched as Georgia's life slipped slowly away, talking to her, telling her it was okay to go. It was her time. Her family would meet her on the other side.

A little over an hour after they removed the machines, she took her last breath and her heart rate dropped slowly to zero.

She was gone.

I was glad I was there for her. A strange peacefulness came over Vanessa and me. It is never easy to watch a loved one die, but we were glad we had those last few moments as a family. The date was October 10, 2003. Georgia was 55 years old.

She wished to be cremated, which allowed me to schedule a service a little later than the customary three days. I decided on the following Saturday, which would give me a week to prepare and would allow co-workers to attend. I wrote a brief eulogy. I didn't really want to speak, but none of the attendees had ever met Georgia. I needed to explain her life to them.

I managed to get through it, not crying until the end when I said, "And now I say goodbye."

Two days after Georgia passed away, I did an internet search for widow/widower support groups. I joined three, one of which was active. The active group was called Youngwidows2 in Yahoo Groups. There I told my story and was greeted by other members, each of them telling about their own loss. Hearing these stories made me realize I was not alone and that things could have been much worse; some of the members had experienced losses that left them financially ruined.

The group became my second home. Every night I would read all the emails, welcome new members, and offer my support to those who needed it. The members are a family, thrown together by the loss of a loved one. If a member has a bad day, all they have to do is email the group, and offers of support come pouring in. I have never belonged to a group where members give their private phone numbers out so freely. I've had the opportunity to meet many of them, and in May of this year I married Ginny, a wonderful woman from our group whose husband died from the same complications as Georgia, also from years of alcohol abuse. I believe

I knew I was going to be OK when I met Ginny for the first time. We get along so well together.

The first time Ginny came to the house I had shared with Georgia, a few strange things happened.

We were in the kitchen. As I embraced Ginny, over her shoulder I watched a magnetic clip with a note attached begin to slide slowly down the side of the refrigerator. That clip had been hanging in the same spot for several months and had never moved. Ginny and I were several feet away and had done nothing that would have caused it to slide. I moved the clip back to the spot it had been in and it hasn't moved in the eight months since.

Later that evening, she and I were sitting on the sofa. I reached out to hug her, and as out arms wrapped around each other a snow globe began to play the song, "New York, New York."

The snow globe had been a gift to Georgia the Christmas before. It was one of her favorites. That snow globe had been moved from Ohio to New Jersey, bounced around from place-to-place, and moved from one spot to another in this house. A good friend helped me decorate the living room a month after Georgia died.

She put the snow globe on a shelf in my entertainment center. It sat there for three months, and the minute I hugged Ginny it played enough notes for anyone to figure out it the song it played.

Both incidents happened just as I hugged Ginny.

Those were the only signs we saw until May. On the evening of our wedding day Ginny was standing in the kitchen. Her back was turned away from an open door, which leads to the garage, laundry room, and the rec room. She heard a noise and turned to watch the door close. We have tested the door since then, and you have to give it quite a push to make the latch click. There were no windows open, and no one had entered or left the house.

When Ginny told me about it, my first thought was, "Georgia left. She knows I am married and content so she feels she can go now." I think she let us know in the only way she could.

The best advice I can offer to the newly bereaved is to seek support among your peers. Most widow/widower support groups have members older than those in our group. We range from the early twenties to early 50's. It is more comforting to be among those in the same age bracket.

Once I found my support group, I found what I could not do alone. I found support and best of all, the ability to put aside my own pain and console others.

And I found Ginny.

Mike Smith is 45 years old and lives in Fort Lee, New Jersey with his new wife, Ginny, and his 17-year-old son. His 19-year-old daughter attends university in Ohio. Mike and his family are originally from Nova Scotia, Canada. Mike works in the telecommunications industry and in his spare time he writes and rides his bicycle.

SOUL MATES

By Paula Meyers

When you are sorrowful look again in your heart, and you shall see that in truth you are weeping for that which has been your delight.

Kahlil Gibran

Scott Meyers and I were high school sweethearts. We started dating when he was a senior and I was a junior. Both our mothers worked in the cafeteria, and they encouraged Scott to ask me to his prom. Thus began our 17 years together.

Scotty was a smoker with occasional high blood pressure, but he always took his medicine and was generally in good health. He was a volunteer firefighter and was active in sports, so we never suspected what was to come.

We were married in 1998 and our son was born in 2000. During this time, Scott's father was on the heart transplant list, but we never knew why. We just assumed it had something to do with his diabetes. (Scott's parents divorced when he was four years old; he lived with his mother and didn't have much contact with his father.)

Scott had always taken naps, but at the beginning of 2003 things were different; he seemed to become aggravated easily, he started getting chest pains (he thought it was heartburn), and he would get short of breath very easily. He went to the doctor and was put back on high blood pressure medicine. He also had an EKG done, which came back normal. His cholesterol was also normal.

Because he was a 34-year-old firefighter who smoked cigarettes, his doctor thought his lungs could be causing the problems. The doctor decided to officially rule out trouble with Scott's heart and scheduled a stress test for June 23. Scott made sure on the 22nd that he had a haircut and on the 23rd he insisted I go to work. He told me he loved me and I told him to call me when the test was over. He said, "Unless the doctor calls first."

I went to work and one hour later received the dreaded phone call from my mother-in-law. She said the hospital had called her and we needed to get to another hospital immediately. I remember speeding down the Pennsylvania turnpike thinking, "I'm too young to be a widow. "

We were taken to the family room of the cath lab, and the hospital chaplain came to pray with us. The doctor came in and told us that Scott had collapsed during the stress test and never regained consciousness. After the autopsy, we discovered that Scott had coronary artery disease and would have needed a heart transplant. At 34, his heart was worse than that of a 90-year-old.

Now I'm a 33-year-old widow, raising our 4-year-old son, Cameron, alone. Because coronary artery disease is hereditary, Cameron has been tested and will be examined again at age seven. We learned after Scott died that his grandfather died from CAD & his father also has it—thus, his need for a heart transplant.

A couple of strange things happened immediately after Scott died. He passed away on a Monday, and the viewing started Wednesday. From Wednesday on, the phone in my house only worked when we were at the funeral home. When we would come home and pick up the phone, you could hear static. We would yell, "Scott, stop it!" and then the phone would work. I live in a five-house row, and the phone company said there was a bee's nest in the box and it was only affecting my phone. Scotty knew I hated to be on the phone.

On Tuesday evening, I told Cameron about his dad; he was wondering why people kept hugging and kissing him. Monday night, the day Scott died, I was turning off the light in my bedroom with Cameron in my arms. Cameron looked into the room and said "Good night, Daddy."

I have had instances where I wake up suddenly because I hear Scott whistle, shake the coins in his pocket or call my name. I have also had four "visits" from Scott during my dreams; the first one is the best, so I'll save it for last.

The second visit occurred three months after Scott died, when Cameron broke his arm. We were at Camp Lejeune, North Carolina visiting my brother, and I was really stressed. That evening I asked Scott for help and during my dream he walked up to me and gave me a hug.

The third visit was after a brother firefighter died (around the five-month mark). Scott came to me in my dream and said he was sorry he hadn't been around lately, but he had been busy. That night I had asked him in my prayers where he had been because I hadn't seen him in awhile.

The last "visit" I had happened on the evening after April Fool's Day. In this dream, I was walking towards the kitchen & Scott was walking past me and said, "Surprise! I didn't die. April Fool's."

Each of these dream visits was in color, and when I awoke, I could remember every little detail.

The first and most remarkable "visit" occurred about a month after Scott died. In the dream, Scott was driving my car through our home town, and we were talking, when he turned to me and said, "I need to show you something." The next thing I know, we are sitting on the steps of a sunken living room in some woman's house. She couldn't see us. Scott showed me this woman sitting on a chair. There was a table with cancer medicine on it beside her. I can't tell you the names of the medicine, but somehow I knew what they were.

All of a sudden this beautiful little girl came running down the steps, ran around the woman, and back up the steps. You could hear her upstairs while we were watching the woman. After the little girl went upstairs, Scott turned to me and said, "I'll be right back." He didn't walk up the steps like a human figure—he floated up the steps, like energy, or a glow. Suddenly, you couldn't hear the girl anymore, and I felt Scott's energy come back down the steps and past me to the woman. The woman started crying hysterically, and Scott's energy enveloped the woman until she calmed down. Then he sat back down beside me and said, "This is what I do now."

I would like to be read by a psychic medium someday. I went to see psychic medium John Edward when he came to Pittsburgh, but I wasn't read. I believe it was because Scott's brother was at a fire call and Scott was with him, not me. I say this because the woman in line in front of me had a reading, and there were just a lot of coincidences that day.

I was told by a remarkable grief counselor that grief is not a sickness and you don't get over it like you do a cold. I don't believe there are distinct and progressive steps to the grieving process; the process is more like a wave, and the reason you're at the bottom of the curl is going to be different each time.

I do agree that the first thing you experience is denial—that's the first emotion when you hear about the death. After that, the steps vary, and yes, you can experience each one more than once.

In the beginning of the grieving process, you are in a sort of fog—you are alive, but not completely. It's as if your body is protecting you while you are riding the waves of grief. At some point along the way—for me it started about eight months after Scotty died—you realize you're not reliving the exact day & time of his death. This will be the beginning of the fog lifting.

Before Scotty died, it would take me awhile to fall asleep at night—my brain would start planning the next day. After his death, I would fall asleep immediately, either from pure exhaustion or from crying. One evening around the 10-month-mark, I couldn't fall asleep right away, and I started planning the next day, week, etc. That's when I realized the fog was lifting, and it was then that I accepted the fact he was gone and wasn't coming back.

I attended, with my mother-in-law, a grief support group that was open to anyone who lost a loved one. I still attend a local young widow/er support group sponsored by the local hospital—this has been extremely helpful. I also belong to a young widow/ers group on Yahoo—this has truly been a Godsend.

I'm also doing several things to help myself through the process. In the beginning, I read numerous books on grief; I think I was searching for someone to tell me I wasn't going crazy. I keep a notebook of stories about Scott that I'm saving for Cameron & I have an angel journal that I write in whenever I feel the urge. Now I find myself searching out books about angels and the after-life. I guess at this point I just want to reassure myself that Scott is okay and someday I will see him again.

I believe I am religious, although I don't attend church. I feel that I can speak to God in my house just as well as I could in church. I say my prayers every night—I pray to God and my angels, and I talk to Scott. I believe that my friends, family, and various support groups have helped me through the grieving process as much as my religion. My mantra from the day he died until the fog lifted was, "Take one day at time!!"

That's the best advice I can give anyone who experiences the death of their soul mate.

WHEN "TILL DEATH US DO PART" DOES

By Saramina Berman

To live in hearts we leave behind is not to die.

Thomas Campbell, "Hallowed Ground"

I write this on the first anniversary of my husband's death. I was 19 years old when we met, 20 when we married, 65 when he died.

We started out as pen pals. Towards the end of World War II, his name and APO number were given to me by my civilian brother-in-law who was classified undraftable, or 4F. In those days, writing to a soldier—especially a soldier overseas, fighting his way from Omaha Beach across occupied France and Belgium into Nazi Germany, as this soldier was reputedly doing—was an act of patriotism for a young woman left behind on the home front. Even if the soldier were a stranger, it was not only proper to correspond with him, it was expected.

So the soldier and I exchanged a couple of letters before V-E Day, May 8, 1945, immediately after which he was shipped back to the United States with his unit to be redeployed for the oncoming invasion of Japan. During the two-week leave he was given between theaters of war, we met face-to-face.

It was love at first sight.

We used the word "forever" a lot, and we used it with an abiding confidence that "forever" was ours merely for the asking. I did not know then, as I do now, that "forever" means being fortunate enough to exit this life together. It does not mean that one of us gets very sick and dies, leaving behind the healthy other.

My family and friends are generally amazed at how well I look. Some are also amazed that I don't move out of the big house we lived in and loved together, that I don't go back to work, that I travel so much and never stay long in one place, that I see a therapist, that I would often rather be alone, and on and on. Even those who so supportively advised, "Don't do anything hastily," are now astonished at something I do or don't do. I call them my "Greek Chorus."

In my present stage of mourning, I easily interpret my Greek Chorus's astonishment as criticism. This perceived criticism demoralizes me. Over the past decade or so, with great effort and considerable professional help, I have been able to separate myself from the psychological dominance of first, a loving, authoritarian, workaholic father, and then a loving, authoritarian, workaholic husband; however, severe stress still has the power to pull me back to old ways and uncertainties.

When I am not immobilized by the sadness of my loss, my energies this past year have been spent internalizing the knowledge that what really matters is what my judgments are, what I choose to do each time I must make a decision from among all my viable options. In my good moments, I am able to let the Greek Chorus's amazement/criticism remain its own, not mine. And I have learned that the only thing I can have "forever" is myself.

To be accepted as a woman alone, willing and able to take care of oneself, is a Herculean task in our society.

Over this past year, I have experienced too many incidents to be misreading the rules. For widows and other single, female adults, the rules are clear: be seen and not heard; don't rock the boat; don't have needs that are new or evolving or different; don't remind us of what we don't want to deal with in our own lives: our own mortality, our own losses, our own vulnerability.

Most widows are senior citizens. Our diminishing capacities are paralleled by the developing ones of the very young. As a widow who wants to take care of myself, from driving my own car rather than being picked up and delivered on someone else's schedule, to signing up for another college degree instead of auditing assorted courses, I have the sense that I am swimming against the tide. Succeeding has become an important part of my grieving process.

Recently I was invited to a wedding in another city. It was the first marriage for the groom, the second for the bride. Together, my husband and I had attended her first wedding. This and a million other excuses surfaced, compelling me not to go. Surprisingly, the idea of not going was no comfort at all. Inside my head, I pushed and pushed myself. I asked the advice of those members of my support network who, from past experience, could be counted on to refute any excuses I might dream up for refusing such an invitation. Finally, with strength I did not know I possessed, I assembled my game plan, including choosing an outfit sufficiently me (not my Greek Chorus) to wear to the wedding, I went.

It was a watershed experience. I felt in charge of myself from beginning to end. After the ceremony and dinner, when the dancing and romantic music became too much for me to bear, I got up, said my good-byes and retired to the safety of my hotel room. It had been a surprisingly successful experiment. I admit I enjoyed myself.

Three people at the wedding, all strangers to me, wished me to "get lucky," meaning that I would meet an eligible man and remarry. I couldn't believe their audacity! Nor can I believe how off the mark that wish resounds for me. I have already gotten lucky. I have survived the monumental loss of the man, not without his hang-ups, who could "take my breath away" during all those years. And in the process of learning to survive without him, I have found the rest of me.

Almost another year has passed since I began this writing. I sold the big house and moved into the newest, swankiest apartment I could afford. The verdict is not in. It may prove to have been too big a leap.

Paradoxically, my sadness now is deeper, more profound, and yet immobilizes me less. I have found new ways of working through the dark feelings. Metaphors, not excuses, surface now to help me deal with difficult times. For instance: what I have been doing these past two years is reconnecting in all my relationships. I have been a train derailed. Some of the railroad cars survive intact, some need the smallest amount of salvage work, and some will never hook on again. In those lost relationships, my husband was the cement that held us all together. Brand-new railroad cars are now being added to replace those which cannot be repaired.

Just as surely as derailed trains do get back on track after proper adjustment, I am getting back to satisfactory functioning. To my great surprise, I find myself laughing more than crying. While life is stingy and precarious about "forever," it is generous and trustworthy about moving on with a flow of its own.

Saramina Berman describes herself as a "late bloomer." She received her Bachelor's degree in Liberal Arts from the University of California at Riverside at the age of 49. She then obtained a teaching certificate and taught school in California before moving to St. Louis, where she earned two Masters degrees—including one in Social Work— in three years from Washington University in St. Louis. Saramina is a retired licensed clinical social worker and a volunteer docent at the St. Louis Holocaust Museum. She also served as an interviewer for the Steven Spielberg Shoah Foundation.

Life's Journey

By Shanna Hugie

*While we are mourning the loss of our friend,
others are rejoicing to meet him behind the veil.*

John Taylor

My husband, Terry Hugie, and I were best friends. We were married for 24 years and have four children. Terry was strong, healthy, full of life and dreams. Then, in April of 1999, he was diagnosed with mylodysplastic syndrome; in June of that year, we learned he had leukemia. He died just one year later.

Right until the moment Terry slipped into a coma we believed that he would make it. It was tough watching him go from vital and young to seeing him hooked up to a ventilator and looking like he was 85 years old when he was only 47. Since his death, the biggest challenge has been facing everything alone and having to be strong for our children <u>all</u> the time. Not being able to just talk to him face-to-face or ever be hugged by him again is the hardest thing of all.

Although I understand that some people benefit from counseling or joining support groups when their spouse dies, I didn't do either. Terry didn't believe in counseling, so my children felt we would be betraying him if any of us sought that type of assistance. Instead, I looked within myself. I write a lot of poetry and that has helped a lot. I also perform 365 "secret service acts" (some people call them "random acts of kindness") a year. I believe these acts only count if I don't get caught, so if I do get caught, I do more. Some examples are: washing the windshields of cars parked in handicapped stalls (my favorite!); sending anonymous notes to store clerks and their managers thanking them for excellent service; leaving flowers on porches of widows and then ringing the doorbell and running; praying for someone; leaving cookies for the mailman (this one isn't secret, but it lets the mailman know he's appreciated); shoveling snow in the winter and mowing lawns in the summer for elderly neighbors or someone who's out of town.

I have a strong religious faith. I am deeply committed to my Heavenly Father and my older brother, Jesus Christ. My beliefs did not just help me get through the grieving process—they were totally what got me through—I could not have survived without my faith. I talk to Terry and to my Heavenly Father all the time. I believe they are very near and love us very much. The trouble is, I believe they also see me when I fall apart, and I wish I could prevent that. I want them to be proud of me.

I look at grief as a very personal journey. While there are specific, defined steps, it's not a one-time trip. You will re-visit that pathway again and again. Think of it this way: If you had a job in a large city and had to walk up stairs to get to your office, you would do that day after day after day. You would never think of it as backsliding, but merely as facing a new day. Thus, it is safe to say that sometimes you will "re-visit" the steps of grief over and over again, sometimes several times in one day. And, just like when you were a child, sometimes you can jump over a step one time, only to find yourself on that step the next time you make a journey.

When your spouse dies, many people want to be supportive, but they don't know what to do or what to say. And they think that by not discussing it, they are helping you "go on." What they don't realize is that you really need to be able to talk about it. Putting it away is kind of like throwing away the person you've lost—people need to let you have your memories and deal with your loss.

Friendships change after a spouse dies, too. I've had women who used to be my friends warn me to "stay away" from their husbands, even though such a thing never occurred to me. I don't seem to fit in with old friends anymore, so I've focused on spending more time with my family and on developing a better "me."

This has been the hardest journey of my life. One important thing I learned on the road to recovery is to take life just five minutes at a time. I find it's imperative to never look more than five minutes ahead; I can do anything for five minutes.

People who have lost loved ones are heroes simply for not giving up and just going on as well as they can. Sometimes the most you can do is brush your teeth and go back to bed. Other times you make great strides. Each step is progress—you aren't competing with anyone—you are merely surviving and enduring to the end. People who tell you to "get over it" need to understand that it is a PERMANENT loss, and you don't "get over" permanent—you just go on.

And—know that you WILL have joy again in your life. Then the trick is not to feel guilty for being happy. The last few years since Terry's death have definitely been challenging. We have had more joy and many, many more trials . . . but the point is, we are still here each new morning and still can recognize the sunrise.

My advice to those going through this life-altering experience is this: "Remember, life is very, very short. I believe we will see our loved ones once again, and that they are doing great and wonderful work on the other side. You, as the survivor, have more living to do—that's why you're still here. Live fully so you will be able to share the wonder of your life with your loved ones when you see them again."

Shanna Hugie is the mother of four—two girls and two boys. Her family has grown to include a son-in-law, daughter-in-law, a grandson and a granddaughter. Shanna writes poetry and looks for her husband's presence in rainbows and sunsets, and sees his smile in the faces of their posterity.

Courage for a New Day

By Sheila Moss

Truly, it is in darkness that one finds the light, so when we are in sorrow, then this light is nearest of all to us.

Johann Echkart

As I sat by my husband's bedside in the hospital emergency room, I talked to him, not knowing whether he could hear me. I was trying to say all the things you want to say to the person you've shared life with for 29 years.

My name is Sheila and I live in Nashville, Tennessee. I work downtown and always commuted to work with my husband, David. When he dropped me off at work on the morning of May 4, I kissed him goodbye as usual. I didn't know that it was goodbye forever.

Late that afternoon, David was caught in a sudden thunderstorm; his car skidded on the wet pavement and collided with another car. Unaware of what had happened, I finished work for the day and left the office to wait for him to pick me up. I waited and waited but he never came. I called his office, but there was no answer. Finally, I called home and found a message from the hospital. My world changed forever.

David died early in the morning on May 5, 1990, without ever regaining consciousness.

By the next afternoon, I was strangely calm, doing the things that had to be done. I went through the motions of calling work, calling family and making funeral arrangements. I was in shock, but didn't realize it then.

The funeral is a blur. I could scarcely believe how many people knew David. It was a military funeral; he was in the military reserves, so I knew that's what he would want. It was a nice funeral—if a funeral can be nice. After it was over, I took the flag from his coffin and returned home.

I knew I was going through a major crisis and I should probably talk to someone, so I made an appointment with a counselor. After several sessions, he recommended I see a grief counseling specialist. I put the specialist's card in my purse, never intending to call. I didn't need help; I was okay. I didn't feel anything. I later learned that shock and denial help us survive pain that would otherwise be overwhelming.

The shock finally started to wear off after a month or two. Reality pounded me with crushing blows. David was dead. He was not coming back.

I held myself together at work, but cried all the way home and all evening, every evening. It is amazing how little sleep a person can actually get by on and still function. I had no appetite; I scarcely ate and eventually would lose over 30 pounds.

I alternated between depression and anger. I was angry with myself for not being able to handle all the paper work and legal business resulting from a death. I was angry at the life insurance company. I didn't want money—I wanted my husband. I was angry because everyone else had a normal life, and my life wasn't worth living. But while some people express anger at God for taking their loved one, I never really directed my anger towards God. I needed all the resources I could find to help me get through this. Most of all I was angry with David because he died and left me alone.

Death is so final and can come so fast. Why did this happen to me? I couldn't figure out what I could possibly have done to deserve this much pain. One day everything had been normal. The next day my world turned upside down. Why had a good person died while less worthy individuals continued to live and thrive? Death follows no logic. It just happens.

Grief masquerades as depression. I would see someone on the street that looked like David and for an instant, I was sure he was alive. I expected to wake up one day and find that this was all a bad dream. Sometimes I simply sat alone with my thoughts and stared into space, losing track of time.

I was grieving the loss of my life mate and the father of my three children, the loss of my hopes and dreams, and the loss of a future together. I have never felt so alone. I had come face-to-face with mortality. I felt as if I were dying, and I really didn't care.

One especially bad day, I remembered the card I had tossed into my purse and decided to call the grief counselor. "I need to come today," I said. I knew a good psychologist would find time for someone who was desperate and he did.

The psychologist was undoubtedly the kindest, most caring person I have ever met. We talked about David and our life together, about my feelings and fears, and about grief. Most important, we talked about the fact that what I was experiencing was normal, and I was not going crazy.

Eventually, when I was far enough along in recovery, the counselor recommended that I find other people who cared and understood what I was going through. But where could I find such people? He recommended a grief support group. I wasn't convinced, but I attended a session and it was the best thing I could have done. Everyone there was going through exactly what I was going through, feeling exactly what I was feeling and thinking that they were crazy, too.

I prayed for strength just to survive. I tried getting through just one day at a time. I felt that I wasn't strong enough by myself, but with the help of a greater power, perhaps I could make it.

I wished for a sign from beyond that David was okay, wherever he was. A month or so after he died, I dreamed of him lying on a slab. Although he was dead in the dream, he groaned as if in great agony and turned over. A ringing phone woke me; it was my son calling about a sudden personal emergency. It could have been mere coincidence, but I felt as if my husband somehow knew and was trying to tell me.

Grief is a journey. During those early days, I sometimes felt lost or sidetracked. When I was suffering, I wanted my journey to go by faster so that I could hurry and get to the end of the pain. But I learned that a person must travel through grief at their own pace, feeling the pain before reaching recovery. A grief journey cannot be hurried.

If there was one thing that helped me towards acceptance, it was something my counselor said that I only appreciated later. He said recovery is a choice; some people choose not to get over grief. I had to choose to recover. Recognizing that I had a choice gave me back some control over my life.

A year went by before I was able to accept my status as a widow and to feel just a little bit better. It seemed to correspond to the old belief of observing a year of mourning after a death. Moving to complete acceptance was a gradual process of adjustment. It was almost three years before I felt close to normal again.

If I were asked to advise a newly bereaved person, I would tell them the pain they are feeling won't last forever. They shouldn't feel that they have to be strong. We have been wounded. It's okay to be weak and let others help us. We need to be kind to ourselves and not expect to recover too quickly. Like any injury, grief needs time to heal.

Eventually, good things come from any life experience, even one as tragic as the death of a spouse. In my experience, I found I had more strength than I ever imagined. I learned to manage alone, and renewed my independence. I made new friends, developed different relationships and learned to live life alone and depend on myself. I also became a far more compassionate person than ever before.

Death of a spouse is one of the worst things that can happen to anyone. It happened to me and I survived. Life will never be the same, and I will always carry the scar. But I've found that it's possible to make a new life and to find courage for a new day.

Sheila Moss is a humor columnist from Tennessee. Her writing includes comedy about big hair, junk cars, country music and football, so writing about a serious topic is a wide departure from her usual fare. She has published several articles and her column appears weekly in several newspapers.

THE RIGHT ONE

By Sue Gutman

What the heart has once owned and had, it shall never lose.

Henry Ward Beecher

I met Alan at a bar in New Jersey in September, 1982. He was the first guy I met in a bar whom I gave my correct phone number to. I just had a feeling he was the right one. He called me a few days later, but I wasn't home. My parents were pretty strict with us girls when it came to dating and calling guys, so I had to sneak over to a friend's house to call him back. Later, Alan told me he probably wouldn't have called again if I hadn't returned his first call. It was meant to be!

On Valentine's Day, 1984, Alan and I were married. We had a wonderful marriage and had three beautiful daughters. Before the birth of our second child, Alan's mother was diagnosed with cancer and given two months to live. At the time of her diagnosis, I had just suffered my second miscarriage, so it was a very difficult time for our family. To make matters worse, Alan was laid off from his job as an electrician. He started a consulting business from our home, working a lot of late hours and traveling quite a bit just so we could keep our home. We had also taken on a great deal of debt during his mother's illness helping to pay her rent and hospital expenses.

After his mother died, our two younger daughters were born and we started putting our finances back in order. It was a much happier time. Alan accepted a job in Indiana, and we moved there from Virginia in 1994. We lived in Indiana for one year before Alan accepted another job—this time in Appleton, Wisconsin.

We didn't necessarily like living in Indiana, but as a family it was a wonderful time. Alan's job was within five minutes of our house, so he was home early every evening and we had a lot of quality family time. When I look back, I realize that this is about the time Alan started exhibiting symptoms of his cancer.

On Christmas Day that year, he complained of pain in his jaw and teeth. A day or two later, he saw a dentist who couldn't find anything wrong, but gave him medicine for the pain. It cleared up. The following spring, Alan shaved his winter beard and noticed a white patch of skin on the jaw line that had not been there before. He also had a white patch of hair on one eyebrow. Later we learned these were symptoms of melanoma, although no one would have been able to diagnose what was happening then.

That summer, 1995, we joined my family on the outer banks of North Carolina. My family still speaks of that vacation very fondly, believing we were given a gift.

We had arranged to rent a basic cottage. As the first renters of the season, when we arrived, the real estate company told us our cottage was uninhabitable. It seems a family of possums had moved into the air conditioning ducts and died sometime during the winter. The rental company set us up in a different house, one that we would never have considered renting otherwise. It was magnificent! There were five bedrooms and 4-1/2 baths, each with a Jacuzzi tub. There was also a hot tub on the deck. It was total luxury—the best vacation ever!

In the fall, Alan and the girls and I packed up yet again and moved to Wisconsin. We loved it there—Alan was happy with his job, the kids were thrilled with the neighborhood, and I loved the people and the shopping. We arrived at the end of September, and by mid-October, Alan was once again experiencing the pain in his jaw.

He found a dentist who saw him quickly. This time, the dentist noticed a mass growing in Alan's mouth and treated it with antibiotics, believing it to be an infection. After two weeks with no improvement in Alan's condition, the dentist sent him to an oral surgeon. By this time, his face was swelling, and I was beginning to worry that something was seriously wrong.

When Alan arrived at the oral surgeon's office and opened his mouth, the doctor nearly fell to the floor. He scheduled a biopsy for the next morning. The biopsy indicated a malignancy, but the type of cancer couldn't be determined. It was then sent to Minnesota for further testing.

While awaiting the results of the biopsy, we were introduced to a wonderful oncologist who immediately began running blood work and CT scans of Alan's face and head. Because the malignancy appeared to be extremely aggressive, the doctors began talking to us about surgery. The surgery couldn't be done until all the test results were in, and what they described would have totally disfigured Alan's face.

Within a few days, the results started pouring in. The Minnesota tests determined the malignancy was a rare form of cancer—amelanotic (non-pigmented) melanoma. The white patches of skin and hair were symptoms. The blood work results showed abnormal liver cells. Surgery was no longer an option.

By this time, Alan had been admitted to the hospital and began aggressive chemotherapy. CT scans of the liver showed that the cancer had spread there. At this point, the doctor was not optimistic. He explained that any measures taken might buy us time, but there was no cure. We were given a two-to-six-month time frame.

Alan decided to undergo the recommended treatments including chemotherapy and large doses of radiation. Radiation, which could only be performed on his face, caused blistering throughout his mouth. During the last week of radiation, the blisters were so bad that he couldn't eat or speak. Side effects from the chemotherapy also started around this time. It was miserable time for all of us.

After two months of treatment, the cancer in the liver was still growing. We made the decision to move back East to be with our family in New Jersey and seek help from the melanoma specialists at Sloan-Kettering Hospital in New York. Our oldest daughter was in second grade, and this would be her third school in a year. She was devastated to have to start over again, but she was a real trouper.

We arrived in New Jersey in February of 1996. Alan was glad to be able to get me and the children back with family. We moved into my parents' home and my father helped out by taking Alan into the city for treatment. The doctor at Sloan-Kettering referred us to a local doctor who could administer the treatments so we wouldn't have to make the trip each week. The cancer was still winning.

By April, the doctors recommended that we stop treatments. Alan had lost more than 80 pounds and was extremely weak. They suggested I keep him home and use hospice care to keep him as comfortable as possible. The last couple of weeks of his life were the most difficult. It was time for us to admit the end was near. Until now, we hadn't even admitted that there would be an end; we still had not given up hope that a miracle would happen.

Alan was only 35 years old; I was 33 and our children were eight, four and three. His death was unthinkable. It's true what they say: you hear about bad things happening to other people, but never think they'll happen to you. Alan and I had been living in a fairy tale world and now we were in the middle of a nightmare. I lay in bed at night praying that God would let me wake up and have the nightmare be over.

Living through something this horrible really grounds a person. You come to realize how much of life is taken for granted. I never fully appreciated what having a great marriage and a wonderful husband meant to me until Alan was gone. Being a widow and raising three children by myself is very lonely. Finding another person with the qualities Alan had will take a miracle.

Religion became an issue between us during Alan's final weeks. I was having a very difficult time with anger and blaming God until one night when Alan and I were talking about it. He looked me in the eye and said, "You can't lose your faith now. Where would that leave me when I go?" I will never forget that conversation. Since that time, whenever I feel the questions coming back to haunt me, I remember those words.

Up until the last week, Alan was still able to function and communicate. It seemed like he took a turn for the worse overnight. Even the hospice nurse was surprised at how quickly he declined. It was time to put things in order and face the fact that the end was near. We still hadn't discussed funeral arrangements. During Alan's lucid moments, I was able to determine where he wished to be buried, and on May 29, I purchased the plot.

Alan died around 1:30 a.m. on May 30. I wish I could say he died peacefully in his sleep, but he didn't. He fought to the end, and finally lost. I actually prayed that night for God to take him. I couldn't handle watching him suffer anymore.

Throughout his illness, I never saw Alan have a moment of self-pity. All his thoughts were of me and the girls and how we needed to continue living after he was gone. The only regret he voiced was that he would miss so much of their growing up. Every now and then whenever the girls start a new adventure or they're all dressed up to go somewhere, I choke up, realizing how much he has missed these past eight years. It's bittersweet to see bits of him in their faces and personalities and not be able to share with him they joy they give me.

After Alan's death, I definitely had moments when I felt his presence. The first time it happened was the morning after he died. I was sitting at the kitchen table on the second floor of my parents' home at around 5 a.m. A bird came to the window and stopped mid-flight for several seconds and stared right at me. I had goose bumps from head to toe. I am convinced Alan came to offer me strength, which is exactly what I had just been asking him to do.

The second experience was the night of his funeral. I was lying in bed in the moment before sleep and saw Alan pass through the light into heaven. It was truly beautiful. It helped a great deal to see first-hand that he was okay.

Since his death, the girls and I have moved back to Virginia, but we still visit my parents' home frequently. To this day, whenever we're there, the smoke alarm makes a funny beep and the phone gives an odd short ring sometime during our visit. We always laugh that it only seems to happen when we're there—the engineer at work!

After settling back in Virginia a couple months after Alan died, I joined a hospice-sponsored grief group. It helped to be able to share my experience with others going through the same thing. I have also received help for the children through grief support groups at school and with hospice counselors.

It's still awkward when meeting new people. Most people assume because of my age that I'm divorced. I'm still very uncomfortable having to correct them and explain that I'm a widow. They always get a horrified expression and I'm forever feeling the need to apologize for their discomfort.

Time does heal wounds as they say, and the girls and I have definitely learned to live with and accept what happened. It took several years to go through the process. We still have setbacks, times when the whole situation feels unfair and unreal, but we have survived, and are for the most part healed.

The "Yes" at the End of the Tunnel

By T.J. Banks

Life is eternal, and love is immortal, and death is only a horizon; and a horizon is nothing save the limit of our sight.

Rossiter Worthington Raymond

When Marissa, my wise old soul of a daughter, was very small, she'd ask me, "Is there a 'yes' at the end of the tunnel?" Somewhere, she'd picked up the phrase, "the light at the end of the tunnel" and decided that a little revision was in order. I found myself agreeing with her. A "yes" sounded so much more positive … so much more … well, life-affirming. And those were qualities that I was very much on the look-out for back then. My husband, Tim, had been killed in a car accident, and there I was, a 34-year-old freelance writer with a 3-1/2 year-old daughter to bring up on my own.

The night Tim died, I lay in my bed, staring into the dark. But what I was seeing in my mind's eye wasn't our bedroom with the familiar furniture all shrouded in shadows—it was Tim's body lying on a metal table, being cut into by the coroner's scalpel. The nauseating scene kept playing over and over like a nightmare I couldn't wake up from.

"I can't cry," I gasped at one point to my mother, who had stayed the night. "Everything hurts."

And everything continued to hurt for a long time. The tunnel was very long and very dark in those days. Our comfortable world had been broken apart, and I couldn't even begin to imagine that it would ever come together again ... that there would ever be anyone for me again, the way that Tim had been. We had known each other since 5th grade and had, in a sense, grown up together. He had been my friend, my confidante, and the only lover I had ever known. And now he was gone somewhere I could not follow.

Two weeks after Tim died, I returned home from some errands and went up to my room to lie down. I knew I couldn't sleep, so I figured I'd just rest for a bit in the cool, shadowy room while my mother took care of Marissa downstairs.

Suddenly, out of nowhere, a white-gold light appeared to the left of the headboard. It hung in mid-air, glowing like a flame, deepening in its intensity as I gazed into the heart of it. The light flickered and danced before my eyes, then slowly … ever so slowly … it faded away.

I sat up, amazed. The room, as I said, tended to be a shadowy one, thanks to the huge oak tree shading the window directly from across the bed. In the past, I'd hung crystals in that same window in vain attempts to work a little rainbow magic there. But there was no prism in the window now—only an enormous aloe plant snaking its arms against the panes. Besides, a prism would have cast its rainbows against the walls, ceiling and floor. It wouldn't have conjured up that firefly flame that hung suspended in the air like that … beckoning me … reassuring me.

A little later, my mom and I went for a walk in the cemetery behind the house. Tim had loved that view with all its trees and wildness, and his parents and I had agreed that that was the most fitting place for him to be buried. We paused by the grave and stared: there were huge, jagged cracks in the earth. "Weather conditions," somebody said when we mentioned it later. But I couldn't help remembering an old story about such cracks meaning that the soul had escaped and made its way to freedom …

In the months that followed, all sorts of odd occurrences took place. Nothing quite as obvious as burning bushes or the like—just things that would have had significance to Tim and me. Once, a deer came to the edge of Tim's overgrown vegetable garden and stared at me without fear, her soul meeting mine in gentle greeting. Days later, a hummingbird flew up to me as I stood by the shed, as fearless as the doe had been.

Tim and I shared a love of nature and animals; we'd both been alive to the beauty of a kingfisher standing by a pond or the playful tumbling of river otters. The deer and hummingbird had brought that same magic with them. To me, it was as though Tim were sending messengers who could reach me when no one else could, to let me know that he was still there … that the body I'd loved might be gone but that the quicksilver soul was still vibrantly, lovingly there.

I constantly looked for such moments. They made the grief easier to bear. I wove them into my novel, *Souleiado*, in which I used my heroine's journey back in time as a way of channeling my own grief. But such moments, soul-stirring as they were, couldn't keep the loneliness at bay forever.

I didn't date for four years after Tim's death; yet, I desperately longed for someone to come and fill the hole in my heart. And when I did begin dating, I made for potential relationships like a wanderer in the desert looking for the nearest oasis.

But oases often turn out to be mirages, and I finally took a sabbatical from dating. I was in quest mode again, to be sure; only this time, I wasn't looking for proof that Tim's changeling soul was still nearby or even for a man who could mean to me what Tim had. No, this time I was looking for the "me" who had been buried along with my soul mate.

It was, believe it or not, the harder quest. In the aftermath of Tim's death, I'd been eaten away by the emptiness I felt and had placed my faith in forces and people outside myself. What I hadn't realized was that I was the missing piece: I had been strangely absent from my own life.

I'd taken up running (or "mogging" – part moseying, part jogging, as I preferred to call it) around this time. Gradually, my morning "mogs" had become a sort of running meditation, putting me back in touch with my intuition and feelings, with a new-old self that was vibrant and in love with my life as it was unfolding before me. I no longer focused on the past—the years with Tim—or the future—the days and nights with some hypothetical new person—but on the present, with Marissa and our many animals, my writing, and my gardening.

There would always be an ache, a hole in my heart where Tim was concerned, but I could live with it and even honor it now.

In many tales of enchantment, there's a moment where the heroine must hold onto something, no matter what frightening form it takes. Only when it has appeared in all its nightmarish guises does it turn into the very thing she's been seeking.

So it was for me with my grief. Only when I let myself experience it full-force and did not try to avoid it (as I had with my various "quests"), did I finally find myself ... and the "yes" at the end of my tunnel.

T. J. Banks has written fiction, poetry, book reviews, and essays for numerous publications. A contributing editor for laJoie and a former editorial associate with the Writer's Digest School, she has won awards for her work from the Cat Writers' Association, The Writing Self, and Burbage's, Ltd. In addition to her time-travel novel Souleiado (Five Star 2002), she has also written a novel for young adults, Houdini. T.J. lives with her daughter, Marissa, their cats, and two "rabbits with issues" in Simsbury, Connecticut.

Taking Flight

By Victoria Gray

If we had no winter, the spring would not be so pleasant; if we did not sometimes taste of adversity, prosperity would not be so welcome.

Anne Bradstreet

In February, 1989, my husband, Wayne, had exploratory surgery, revealing cancer that had spread throughout his body. The doctors said he had about three months to live. He died just three weeks later on March 2. He was 69 years old.

To say that my reaction was probably different from most people who suffer the loss of a spouse is putting it mildly. I have always been a very spiritual person. I've always believed that God, the Universe, my angels and spirit guides are with me no matter what happens.

I mention this so that you'll understand what I'm going to say next: When I stepped out of the hospital after my husband's death, I literally saw and felt what appeared to be a heavy, wet wool coat being lifted off my shoulders. For the first time in a long while, I felt free. I had a feeling of complete and total calm.

Wayne had been very controlling, a trait I wasn't aware of until after we were married. I was divorced with two young children when we met. During our 3-1/2 year marriage, I gave birth to two more babies. I also helped out with the janitorial supply company we owned. With all these responsibilities, I was still expected to play a subservient role in our relationship. Not only did I have to prepare his breakfast every morning (fresh-squeezed orange juice everyday, poached eggs, toast and bacon one day, and cereal, toast and bacon on opposite days), he also demanded that I shave his face immediately after breakfast. And on the rare occasions when we ate dinner at a restaurant, he'd insist that we split a meal!

As if all that weren't degrading enough, he set the rules on when and where I was allowed to use our checkbook to pay bills. At the end of each month, Wayne would have my older daughter watch the younger kids and then he'd set up a table stacked with bills, stamps, envelopes and pens in the garage. Then, and only then, was I allowed to write the checks. After filling them out, I'd have to hand them to him for his approval and signature. The fact that I'd been head bookkeeper for a major finance company a few years prior to our marriage, and had closed down my own decorating company in order to relocate with him, made no difference.

Despite sometimes feeling like a prisoner in my own home, I must admit I did have feelings for him. Our relationship may not have been one of equal partners, but it was a relationship nonetheless. So when he died, I had mixed emotions: I was sad and yet relieved at the same time.

At home that night after he died, I sat with my two youngest children on the sofa, holding baby Ashley in my left arm as she nursed, with my right arm around Blake. It was peaceful there in the dark, quiet room. I decided to tell them what had happened. I had never talked down to my children, and had no intention of starting now.

"You know Daddy has been away these past few weeks. And tonight he went on to another life … a spirit life. Your father was very sick and couldn't fight anymore. He won't be coming back home. I wanted to be the one to tell you. He loved both of you so very much." I ended by telling them I wasn't sure what life had in store for the five of us, but that we'd be together no matter what.

I had a gnawing, empty feeling in the pit of my stomach. Would I be able to cope raising four children all by myself? There was no doubt I'd have to continue working; I'd worked all my life. I had managed with two children, but with four … I didn't know how I would do it, but I knew I had no choice.

Although Wayne had died without life insurance, we did have $40,000 in the bank. I was able to stretch that out for a year and a half, even after using $12,000 to buy a much-needed minivan.

I worked from home during the first year, contacting various suppliers for our janitorial company in search of natural cleaning products. I had no way of knowing if there was a connection between chemical products and Wayne's illness, but I no longer wanted anything to do with them. In the meantime, my older daughter, Rachel, convinced me to let her be home-schooled so she could care for her brothers and sister while I worked. The arrangement proved beneficial for all of us. My children have always been close. Rachel still refers to her siblings as "my babies."

I believe that keeping busy (how could I not keep busy with four kids?) and maintaining a positive attitude were instrumental in my survival. I knew in my heart I would get through this challenge, one day at a time.

I often wondered at the suddenness of my husband's illness and death, though. As I mentioned, I've always been spiritual, and I couldn't figure out why he would leave this life so soon after his children were born. Then five years after his passing, I had a dream: I was in an apartment, and Wayne peeked his head around the corner. He said he couldn't stay any longer, and asked me to please take care of his children. Then he was gone. This dream was somehow comforting to me.

My advice to anyone whose spouse has died is to make positive changes. Many newly bereaved people keep their homes exactly the way they were when their spouse was alive. That's a sure-fire way to stay stuck in the past. As the survivor, we need to move forward, to learn to face new challenges. Change is inevitable. It is up to us to choose how to live. We can stay mired in unhappiness or we can choose to live life to its fullest. Try something new, something you wouldn't necessarily have tried while your spouse was still alive. Step off that limb of self-doubt and fly … just fly.

Victoria Gray is a widow and mother of four. She's also a Designer, Real Estate Agent, buyer and seller of estates and an author of three books. She was awarded one of four Women in History awards in March 2002, History month in St. Louis, Missouri. She enjoys reading, writing and taking various classes, which include film making, script writing and cinematography.

A Good Life

Gerry Werner

The only cure for grief is action.

George Henry Lewes

In 1983, we had been married for 37 years. My husband, Hank, had a secure job with the local telephone company, and I was working as an office administrative assistant. Our two children were away at college, and we were finally finding time to do things together. Our second home, a farm house and 72 acres in the country, had been great for the kids and their friends; we had horses and cattle, did float trips and barbecued with friends and family every weekend. Our main home was comfortable. Both of us had nice cars. Life was good.

Then on January 20, shortly after we went to bed, Hank went into ventricular fibrillation. He had just been for a checkup and everything looked good. The paramedics tried to revive him—but he died on the way to the hospital. The doctor termed it "instant death." That has never been an adequate explanation, nor a consolation.

Fortunately for me, I still had my mother, my children and my friends. I thank God for them all. I was still working and got involved in other activities to keep busy.

The same year Hank passed away, my mother fell and broke her hip. After surgery, she came to live with me. She was with me for five years, and in that time, everything that could go wrong when you are on your own did. First, there were the termites. Then the stove caught fire. The roof started leaking and had to be replaced.

Then our station wagon burned up on a trip to the farm. Four adults in one motel room wasn't the problem; it was sneaking a 75 lb. dog in and out that worried me! However, we replaced the motor with a used one to save money; then the car stalled at every stop sign.

The days that followed were busy. I hired a lady to stay with my mother (who never really recovered) during the day and I took care of her at night. The last 2-1/2 years of her life she spent in a nursing home—which still bothers me.

Then I started dating a man I had known for years. This was probably the best three years I'd had in a long time. We knew a lot of the same people; we both liked to travel and once again—life was good.

Unfortunately, he contacted fungal pneumonia, and having smoked heavily all his life only made matters worse. He only lived three months after the diagnosis. Once again, I was alone.

A few years later, a friend of mine introduced me to her widowed cousin. He was a country boy, and we shared a great love for horses. So once again I was able to ride country trails, have a garden, have friends and relatives visit. Again, life is good—right? Wrong! He developed lung cancer (he had smoked when younger). After going through treatment, he lived about a year. The daughter of the friend who introduced us asked her mom if I was the "Black Widow." That didn't boost my morale. I decided to give up on gentlemen friends.

I have moved from the house where I lived for 37 years and now live closer to both my children. I now have four grandchildren. I'm active in church, do a bit of genealogy, have my family for dinner often, and still have my friends of many years, for which I am eternally thankful. They are truly my extended family.

When I look back at my life as a widow, I see that it could have been a lot worse.

I guess you could sum up my philosophy of life in this quote: "Yesterday is history; tomorrow is a mystery; today is a gift; that's why it's called the present."

Gerry Werner is a retired administrative assistant. She lives in St. Louis, Missouri, near her children and grandchildren. She is active in her church and likes to travel, cook and spend time with her family and friends.

Made in the USA
Lexington, KY
30 May 2010